Samuel Cox

**Salvator Mundi**

Or Is Christ the Savior of all Men? Second Edition

Samuel Cox

**Salvator Mundi**
*Or Is Christ the Savior of all Men? Second Edition*

ISBN/EAN: 9783337165307

Printed in Europe, USA, Canada, Australia, Japan

Cover: Foto ©Lupo / pixelio.de

More available books at **www.hansebooks.com**

# SALVATOR MUNDI.

# SALVATOR MUNDI:

OR,

## IS CHRIST THE SAVIOUR OF ALL MEN?

BY

## SAMUEL COX.

"But we trust in the living God, who is the Saviour of all men, specially of those that believe."

SECOND EDITION.

LONDON:
C. KEGAN PAUL & CO., 1 PATERNOSTER SQUARE.
1878.

TO MY BIBLE-CLASS,

WITH MY LOVE.

When man at length his ideal height hath gained,
So that the heavenly kingdom is attained,
Will there be any room for tears and pain,
For dim grey twilights, sobbing wind, and rain,
Mist, wreaths, and flying clouds, the thunder's roar,
Or the sea breaking on a lonely shore,
With all the yearnings these things shadow forth?
Is the pathetic minor but for earth,
And will the heavens resound with joy alone,
Though sadness often makes a deeper tone?
Must all of life fall off that cannot show
Some fruit that did to full perfection grow?
The tottering steps, the pause, even the fall,
Will not eternal life have room for all;
And in the circle of Infinity
Must not all moods of life unfolded lie,
But all complete,—the weak within the strong,
And the one verse become a perfect song;
The bud, the blossom, the fruit-laden bough,
Seen by the light of the eternal *now?*
May not all discords to one concord lead—
Whose every missing note would leave a need
Deep, unimagined as a world untrod—
An infinite harmony whose name is God?

# PREFACE.

The main object of this book is to encourage those who "faintly trust the larger hope" to commit themselves to it wholly and fearlessly, by shewing them that they have ample warrant for it in the Scriptures of the New Testament.

For more than twenty years I have held, and preached, the views advocated in these Lectures; but, in their present form, they were delivered to my Bible-Class only last Winter. Now my Bible-Class is one of which any man might be proud. It consists of more than a hundred-and-fifty members, men and women. Three or four of them are good Biblical scholars, versed in Greek and Hebrew; a large proportion of them, thanks to our Grammar Schools and High Schools, have some slender acquaintance with their Greek Testaments: and all, or nearly all, of them are accustomed to study the sacred Scriptures with intelligence and devotion. At the close of each Lecture I invited the frankest statement of difficulties and objections,—an invitation which provoked a very frank and eager response. Some of the discussions which ensued were very instructive—at least to me; and I often learned from them "where the shoe pinched:" while, sometimes, I not only learned what were the real difficulties in the minds of those who listened to me, but also how they might be met. As far as I could I met them, both at the time and in subsequent additions to or modifications of my manuscript. I would fain hope, therefore, that those who read these Lectures will find that some at least of the difficulties which have obscured their hopes, whether for themselves or for the world at large, have been removed from their path, and that points of view have been opened up to them which they have not heretofore occupied. If that should be so, they will owe something to my Class as well as to myself.

It would have been easy to recast these Lectures into a more bookish form, and thus to have avoided some of the brief recapitulations which will be found in them; but, in the process, they might have lost some of their vivacity; and it would not have been so clear, had these recapitulations been omitted, that the argument is a cumulative one, and needs to be considered as a whole, as well as in its separate parts.

Of all branches of theology Eschatology is perhaps the least attractive to sober and thoughtful students of the Inspired Word, especially if they have discovered that the New Testament predictions of ages and things to come can only be safely approached through the long and winding avenue of Old Testament prophecy. But that section of it which relates to the conditions of men after death is one which so profoundly affects our whole conception both of the character of God and of the salvation wrought by Christ, that even those who most shrink from the interpretation of prophecy are compelled to study it. Indeed I cannot but think it a binding duty on all preachers of the Word that they should not only come to some well-considered conclusion on this point, but that they should also publish and enforce that conclusion, whatever it may be. Few of the more thoughtful and cultivated preachers of the Gospel now hold the dogma of everlasting torment; in a large circle of acquaintance I hardly know one: and yet how few seek to replace it, in the mind of the Church, with any doctrine which they hold to be more in accordance with "the mind of the Spirit." When they are compelled to speak on this point, many are content, not to interpret, but simply to repeat, the very words of Scripture. But, if it be an honest, it is surely an undignified and unteacherlike procedure, to use in one sense words which their hearers take, and which they know their hearers to take, in another and a very different sense. Many plead that they cannot speak out without giving a kind and degree of offence which would close the minds and hearts of most of those who listen to them against their influence, an influence which on the whole tells for good, and which therefore they are not at liberty to sacrifice. But do they not a little forget how much, and what grave, offence they are giving to their more intelligent and inquiring hearers, those who really give the spiritual tone to their Congregations, by their silence, or their equivocation, on a point of such grave importance? Truth may be dangerous, both to him who utters it, and even to those who listen to it. But is it our function, as ministers of the Word, to avoid danger, or to proclaim the truth? and are we so very much wiser and better than our hearers that the truths which are good for us may be highly injurious to them? If any man hold, or is convinced that he holds, any truth, in God's name let him utter his truth or conviction, and leave the consequences with the God who gave it him, and who is quite able both to rule and to save the world without our help, and is not in the least likely to be helped by any man's infidelity to his convictions. The Church is not dying, nor likely to die, of too much truth; but it is sure to languish if its teachers, even for the most amiable reasons, suppress the truth that is in them. And such a truth as *this*—a truth which makes God a just God and a Saviour to us, and the Gospel veritable good news; how can any reasonable man think to serve God by hiding it!

Of those teachers and preachers who honestly retain the dogma which attaches an endless torment to the sins of time no man can ask more than that, while they preach it with sincerity, they also keep their minds open to any more light which may break out upon them from God's holy Word; but of those who have seen that light and yet will not suffer it to shine through their teaching, what can one say but that they are less worthy of their high calling than those who still walk in darkness?

I have read most of the books on the theme discussed in this Volume which have appeared during the last half century; and no doubt am more indebted to some of them than I know. There are but three to which I consciously owe much: (1) A Volume published, I should think, nearly thirty years since, by my friend Mr Dobney of Maidstone, the very name of which I cannot now recall, though I read it eagerly at the time and learned much from it: (2) "The Second Death and the Restitution of All Things," by Andrew Jukes, a valuable and suggestive work which swept the last remnants of difficulty clean out of my mind: and (3) Dr Dewes's too brief remarks on one branch of the subject in his "Plea for a New Translation of the Scriptures." But, on the whole, I believe I may say quite simply and honestly that I have got my views from long study of the New Testament itself, and not from any comments on it.

# CONTENTS.

|     |     | PAGE |
|---|---|---|
| I. | The Question Raised, | 1 |
| II. | The Limits within which it will be Argued, | 19 |
| III. | Damnation, | 36 |
| IV. | Hell, | 55 |
| V. | The Christian Doctrine of the Æons, | 96 |
| VI. | The Christian Doctrine of the Æons, | 117 |
| VII. | The Test and Testimony of Principles, | 144 |
| VIII. | The Universality of Christ's Redemption, | 172 |
| IX. | What we Shall Be, | 193 |

# SALVATOR MUNDI.

## I.—THE QUESTION RAISED.

#### St Matthew xi. 20-24.

"If the mighty works which were done in you had been done in Tyre and Sidon, they would have repented long ago in sackcloth and ashes." Then why were those mighty works *not* done? Is it not the will of God that none should perish, but that all should come, through repentance, unto life? Does not He Himself plead with men, saying, "Why will ye die?" And yet the Lord Jesus, who knew what might have been as well as what had been, solemnly declares that even the guilty inhabitants of Sodom and of Tyre and Sidon *would have been* brought to repentance and life had they witnessed the mighty works wrought in the favoured cities of Galilee! Why were they not permitted to witness them, then? Can we blame them, will God condemn them, and condemn them to an eternal death or an eternal misery, because they did not see what they could not see, because they did not repent, when the very means which would infallibly have induced repentance were not vouchsafed them?

A momentous question this! few questions are more momentous. It is a question which demands an answer, even though we cannot hope, as I suppose we cannot, to reach a full and complete answer to it while we are compassed about with the limitations and infirmities of this hindering mortality. The complete answer would imply a complete apprehension of the entire scheme of Providence, a complete knowledge not only of the whole story of time, but also of the Divine motives and purposes of which that story is a vast and manifold illustration. And such knowledge is too wonderful for us,—too high for us to reach, too broad for us to grasp. But some answer we *must* have, some considerations which at least lighten the burden of this pressing and momentous problem.

First of all, then, let us attempt to lay hold on the words which have raised this problem—to trace out the order and sequence of thought in this suggestive but obscure saying of our Lord's.

In Verse 20 we read, "Then began he to upbraid —to reproach—the cities wherein most of his mighty works were done, because they repented not." *Then!* *When?* When his mind was occupied with the thought (Verse 19) that the Divine Wisdom would be justified of all her children. That Wisdom had sent forth many of her sons to turn the men of Galilee from their sins,—heroes, statesmen, prophets, poets; from the old-world patriarch to the modern rabbi, a long succession of holy men had spoken to them, all delivering the same Divine message, but delivering it in divers manners,—Wisdom changing her modes and tones, and becoming all things to all men, that she might win the more. And last of all, and to crown all, the Baptist had come, and the Messias: John, solitary and austere, keen, incisive, stimulating as the frost of winter; Jesus, sociable, friendly, bountiful, as sweet and genial as a summer's day. But whatever the form which Wisdom assumed, whatever the tone in which she spoke, the men of Galilee found somewhat to allege against her. In her child John she was too austere, too exacting; *he* was a devil of a man, frowning on all the sweet and kindly uses of life. In her child Jesus she was too sociable, too pliable, too ready to condone and to share the indulgences of the worst and most despised of men. *He* had a devil, too, but a gluttonous and wine-bibbing devil, not a solitary and ascetic devil like John's.

This was the attitude which they assumed towards the Divine Wisdom that so graciously strove and pleaded with them, an attitude of captious and yet inveterate hostility. And now Christ sees that men possessed by so settled an hostility to every form of Wisdom and Righteousness as that they translate them into their very opposites, must be nearing the end of their course. As they will not repent and live, let Wisdom change her voice and note as she will, nothing remains but that she should vindicate the children whom they have rejected and condemned, by shewing that it was by her inspiration that they had spoken, and that all they had said on her behalf was true. Those who would not repent unto life when denounced by John and invited by Jesus, and held that they *needed* no repentance, must be left to die; their very death in sin proving that they did need to repent before they could live. As they had left Wisdom no other way of justifying herself, of proving herself to be the true wisdom, and the course she indicated the only wise course, she must take *this* way of justifying both her children and herself.

In Verses 21 and 23, three of the cities in which Wisdom had uttered her voice, and the mighty works of Christ had been done, are named as samples of the other cities of Galilee—Chorazin, Bethsaida, Capernaum. And all these are now mere names to us, and nothing more. So utterly has the prediction of Christ been fulfilled, at least on its lower earthlier side; so intolerable was the judgment which fell on these wicked cities, and so completely were they destroyed.

by it, that it is impossible so much as to identify the very sites on which they once stood. The rocks of Tyre and the harbour of Sidon may still be seen; the place of Sodom is defined by the Sea which destroyed it, the very name of which is, as it were, the epitaph of its inhabitants. But a more intolerable and obliterating judgment has fallen on the cities of Galilee. The place that once knew them knows them no more; no indubitable vestige of them can be traced. We know that they were once busy and growing towns on the teeming north-western shore of Gennesaret; and that is all we can say of them. Some geographers, indeed, have found Capernaum, *i.e.*, the village of Nahûm, in the heap of ruins which the Arabs call Tell Hûm, and Chorazin in the modern Kerâseh, and affirm that Bethsaida stood on both sides the river at the point where the Jordan runs into the lake. But there is no common or general assent to any of these identifications. These ancient cities were sentenced to destruction by the Divine Wisdom to which they had refused to listen; and the sentence has been executed so rigorously, and so long ago, that all trace of them has been lost.

And yet it was not without pain and regret, we may be sure, that Jesus pronounced so heavy a doom on "his own city," Capernaum, in which He had spent many tranquil and many laborious hours; or on the neighbouring towns, which had yielded Him many disciples, and in which He had so often taught and healed. He was a man such as we are; and that which was familiar was dear to Him, as it is to us. I dare say He could have better spared many a better city than either Capernaum or Bethsaida. And there is some trace of this natural pity and regret—there is a sound of sighing in the very sentence He pronounced upon them; for the Greek word (οὐαί), rendered "woe" in the exclamations, "Woe unto thee Chorazin! woe unto thee Bethsaida!" is elsewhere translated "Alas!" and here also it is an expression of pity; for by these exclamations our Lord means nothing less, though He may mean much more, than this: "Unhappy and unblessed are ye, Chorazin and Bethsaida, and I am sad to tell you so!" There is another slight but significant indication of this mood of ruth and pity in the verb with which the Evangelist introduces the "woe." "Then began He to *reproach* the cities," &c.; for we only "reproach" those whom, in some sort, we have loved and trusted, of whom we had hoped better things.

But, though his heart hung with tender compassion over these doomed but familiar cities, Jesus does not hesitate to utter their doom; for Love can be strong and severe even while it is sad and pitiful, and He who loved men much loved God more. And, indeed, it was not *He* who condemned these cities, nor God. They had condemned themselves. He does but utter the sentence which they had virtually passed on themselves—that they were unworthy of eternal life. *Life*, in its true sense, was not in any of their thoughts. They did not aim at a life wisely and righteously ordered, but at a busy, money-getting, self-indulgent life—a life which fits men neither for earth nor for heaven—a life, therefore, which, though it may seem to soar into a very heaven of wealth, success, distinction, enjoyment for a time, is inevitably doomed, and self-doomed, to sink into a hades of ruin and oblivion.

*This* was the condemnation of these cities, that light had come to them, the very Light which is the life of men; and they had loved darkness better than light, because their deeds were evil. But in the mind of our Lord this condemnation took a special and instructive form. If we ask *Him* why He sighs forth sentence against the cities of Galilee, He replies that He condemns them for this, that in this they condemn themselves,—*that the mighty works done in them had not brought them to repentance.* But why should they? What was there to induce repentance in the miracles of Christ? Miracles naturally beget wonder, admiration, awe; but what is the link of connection between miracles and penitence? I apprehend it to be this. Miracles, mighty works, disclose the Divine presence and activity. They shew that God is with men. They bring home to the thoughtful heart a sense of his abiding presence and activity. And how shall sinful men consciously stand in the immediate presence of God without becoming aware of the sins by which they are degraded and defiled? And how should they become profoundly sensible of sin without also becoming profoundly sorry for it? We cannot so much as wake up in the night under the impression that *any* invisible Presence is with us, but we tremble and are afraid, because we feel our unfitness to enter into the world in which our spirits lie open and naked to God and our fellows. And if, as we went about the daily business of life, *God* were suddenly to stand before us, to become visible to us in all the sweetness and glory of his goodness, yet not clothed in the robes of his eternal majesty, would not our first impulse be to fling ourselves at his feet and cry, "Unclean, unclean!" Would not a goodness so pure call up an intolerable and crushing sense of our own impurity? And if He were to lay his hand upon us, and to lift us from the dust of our self-abasement, and to go with us for a little while on our way, should we not walk with Him with a softened, penitent, and lowly heart? *That*, then, was one of the functions—perhaps the main function—of the miracles wrought by Christ.

They were capable of producing, they were designed to produce, so vivid and intense a consciousness of the Divine Presence as should convict men of sin and lead them to repentance.

Just now the set of thought among students of the Bible is to underrate the value of miracles, as in the last century the tendency was to overrate them, or at least to apply them to evidential purposes which they were not intended to subserve. *Then* perhaps men made too much of them; *now* we make too little of them. Science scorns miracles, though she herself has both discovered and wrought many mighty works, and furnished us with many a sign and proof of the Divine presence and activity and goodness. And, to meet the changed attitude of the world around it, Theology is busily engaged in reducing both the evidential and moral force of miracles, in arguing that the unexampled character and the pure morality of Christ are the best proof of the miracles He claimed to have wrought, rather than in arguing that his miracles prove Him to have been sent by God to teach men truth and win them to repentance and righteousness: while Biblical Criticism eagerly undertakes to shew that in the addresses and letters of the Apostles little stress is laid on the miracles wrought by Christ, and great stress on the still mightier truths He enunciated and enforced.

All this may be, I believe it is, in the true line of advance; but perhaps there has been something too much of it. And assuredly the change is not a wholesome one when it leads us to lay so much emphasis on the teaching of our Lord as that we come to forget, or question, or deny the force and value of those supernatural works which were a natural result of the Divine energies which dwelt in Him. To pitch the cargo overboard will, indeed, lighten any ship; but it may also make it ride so high as that it will endure no after storm; and what if, when it does reach the haven, we find that little or nothing of value is left in it? Sceptics of a certain school are forward to compliment the morality of Christ at the expense of his miracles; and, perhaps, with a view to conciliate them and to secure a hearing for Christian truth, we are somewhat too ready to put the question of miracles out of our thoughts, and to insist mainly, if not solely, on the beauty and completeness and spirituality of his teaching and commandments. But have we duly considered what a Christ who wrought no miracle would be to us? and what use those same sceptics would be likely to make of the admission, should any considerable section of the Church ever admit, that the Christian miracles were a late and incredible addition to the New Testament records? Would they not pounce on the admission with eager delight, and forthwith proceed to reduce Christ to the level of other wise men, or men of genius, or even below the highest level of manhood? Might they not reasonably reproach us with the worship we render Him; or even demand how we can hope that any mere man, however gifted, should prove to be the Saviour and Lord of the entire race?

And we—what should *we* not lose? If Christ Himself did not become a dubious historical figure to us, if even his moral teaching did not become uncertain and questionable, we must at least lose both our faith in Him as Son of God, and our hope in Him as Son of Man. For how should the Son of God be in the world, and never do any such creative or restorative work as the Father is ever doing? And if the Son of Man had not power over the phenomenal world, the realm and sequences of Nature, how can we any longer hope that He will restore to us, and to the race at large, that dominion over all the works of God's hands which we feel to be our birthright, and which seems to be the inevitable pre-requisite of spiritual life in its highest and most permanent forms?

Let us remember, then, that Christ Himself saw a moral and spiritual value in the mighty works He wrought in the cities of Galilee; that He even claimed to be believed, if not for his own sake or for the truths He taught, yet for his very works' sake. Let us endeavour, for once, to achieve a feat very difficult to our mental weakness,—that of holding two distinct but complementary thoughts in our minds at one and the same time. The modern set of opinion in the Church, the tendency to subordinate the miracles of Christ to his teaching, is a very healthy one if we do not so far yield to it as to doubt whether those miracles had any moral or religious value to the men who witnessed them, as also, in a lessened degree, for us who do but read of them. To *them* the mighty works brought that sense of the presence and activity of God which induces, or ought to induce, repentance; and to *us* they are of value as shewing that God was once in the world, and that He who was once visibly in the world is always in it and always at work in it, to heal our diseases, to minister to our needs, to quicken us to life everlasting. They feelingly persuade us that Christ was in very deed the Son of the Father; they animate us with the hope that, through the perfect Son of Man, we shall become lords of ourselves and of this lower world, reigning together with Him by whom we have been redeemed.

But behind this difficulty of the miracles, and of the way in which we are to regard them, and the value we are to set upon them, there rises a question still more difficult and perplexing. The man Christ Jesus obviously thought highly of his mighty works, and of their power to open and impress the human heart. In his mind they were not only the great bell of the universe ringing in the world to listen to the sermon He had to preach, but also a part of the sermon itself, and even a very effectual part. He was quite sure that if they had been done in Sodom, and Tyre, and Sidon, these great cities would have repented and remained; and yet Sodom was a synonym for the most utter and bestial corruption, while Tyre and Sidon were among the most flagrantly sensual and vicious communities of the ancient world. Now how those who hold that Christ possessed only human faculties interpret this claim of his to know what men who lived two thousand years before Him *would* have done had their conditions been other than they were; how they explain the fact that He, the most sane, the most modest and unassuming of men, assumed to compare Sodom with Capernaum, Chorazin and Bethsaida with Tyre and Sidon, and to pronounce the wickedest races of heathen antiquity more susceptible to the influences of the unseen spiritual world than the sons of the elect Israel, it is not for me to say; but to me, I confess, this seems to be a monstrous and incredible assumption, at variance with all we know of Him, unless He were what He claimed to be, the Son of God.

Son of God, or Son of Man, He claims to know that

the men of Sodom and of Tyre and Sidon would not have resisted the influences which failed to bring the men of Galilee to repentance and life; and so the question returns upon us, and must no longer be evaded: If these ancient sinners would have repented unto life had the mighty works of Christ been done in their streets, why were they not done?

One answer to this grave question is a very obvious one, and is obviously true so far as it goes. For it is manifest that if God were to come and dwell with men, He could only come once in the history of the world. He could not be for ever coming. There could not be an advent, an incarnation, a life illustrated by mighty works, in every generation, among every race, or the operations of law would have been superseded by a constant miracle or a miracle constantly repeated. And we know so little of the course and order of the world that we cannot venture to say what would have been the best and most fitting time for the manifestation of the Son of God; we are compelled to assume that He, to whom the whole course of time is open and present, chose the fitting conjuncture, that it was, as the Bible affirms, in the very fulness of times that He sent his Son into the world. But if the time of Capernaum, and Chorazin, and Bethsaida was the due and fitting time for this supreme disclosure of the Divine Love and Grace, then obviously it could not have been made two thousand years before. It would have been inconsistent with the scheme and purpose of God, with that economy in the use of miracles which characterizes his government and education of the world, that the mighty works of Jesus should have been done in the ancient cities of the Plain and in the ports and emporiums of the Phœnician coast.

So much we can see, so much we admit. Nevertheless it irks and saddens us to think that even for these ancient and sinful cities God should not have done the most and best that could be done to bring them to repentance. It seems hard and unjust that a man's salvation, a man's life, should hang on the age into which he is born; that the sinners of Sodom, for example, should have had a worse chance than the still greater sinners of Capernaum.

Shall we say then that, although the men of Sodom might have been saved by a gospel they never heard, they nevertheless had all that they needed for salvation had they cared to use the means of instruction and grace which they possessed? I for one cannot say that. I am not unmindful of the fact that had they come into the world some two thousand years later than they did, and walked the streets of Capernaum, and witnessed the works of Christ, they must have accepted all the conditions of that later age, adverse as well as propitious, and might very possibly have been so moulded and so hardened by them as that even then they would not have entered into life. And yet who dare say of any class of men, in any age, that nothing but their own will prevented their salvation? There are thousands and tens of thousands in this Christian land to-day who have never had a fair chance of being quickened into life. Conceived in sin and shapen in iniquity, inheriting defects of will and taints of blood, cradled in ignorance and vice, they have hardly heard the name of Christ save as a word to curse by. And there are thousands and myriads more to whom the faith of Christ has been presented in forms so meagre and narrow, or in forms so fictitious and theatrical, that the only wonder is that so many of them care to worship Him at all. And with all these in our midst now that the Gospel has been preached among us for a thousand years, which of us will dare to affirm that those ancient sinners of Sodom, born in an age so dark, reared in "fulness of bread and abundance of idleness," enervated by a tropical climate and by the abominations amid which they were nurtured, had *all* that men needed in order that they might know the only true God and serve Him alone? Assuredly Lot was no Jesus, no Jonah even, or they might have listened to him and repented; if he "vexed his righteous soul from day to day" with their unlawful deeds, he did not hesitate to risk his soul and the souls of his children by "standing in the way of sinners" to secure a fat inheritance.

No; to say, "Doubtless God gave these poor men all that was necessary to life and virtue," and to make a merit of saying it as though it were a mark of piety, is simply to offer Him that insincere flattery, to shew Him that respect of persons, which even Job could see He Himself would be the first to rebuke, and rebuke the more heavily precisely because it was shewn to *Him*.[1]

What *shall* we say then? For myself I can only say that I see no way out of the difficulty, no single loophole of escape, so long as we assume what the Bible does not teach, that there is no probation beyond the grave, that no moral change is possible in that world towards which all the children of time are travelling. I, at least, am so sure that the Father of all men will do the most and best which can be done for every man's salvation as to entertain no doubt that long ere this the men of Sodom and of Tyre and Sidon *have* heard the words of Christ and seen his mighty works —seen and heard Him, perchance, when He stood and shone among the spirits in the Hadean prison, and preached the gospel to them that were dead, in order that, while still judged according to men in the flesh, they might live according to God in the spirit.[2]

[1] Job xiii. 7-11.      [2] 1 Peter iii. 19, 20; and iv. 6.

And what else, or less, do our Lord's own words imply: "It shall be *more tolerable* for them at the day of judgment than for you?" Lives there the man with soul so dead and brain so narrow that he can take these solemn words to mean nothing more than that the men of Tyre and Sidon will not be condemned to quite so hot a fire as the men of Chorazin and Bethsaida! Must they not mean at least that in the future, as in the present, there will be diversities of moral condition, and a discipline nicely adapted to those diversities? May they not mean that those who have sinned against a little light will, after having been chastened for their sins with a "few stripes," receive more light, and be free to walk in it if they will? We are often chastened in this world that we may not be condemned with the world, often judged and condemned and punished that we may be aroused to repentance and saved unto life everlasting. Why, then, should we always take the chastenings of the world to come to mean judgments, and the judgments to mean condemnations, and the condemnations to mean nothing short of a final and irreversible doom? On the contrary, we ought rather to hope that, while during the brief hours of time our lives describe but "broken arcs," in eternity, and through whatever chastening and discipline may be requisite for us, they will reach "the perfect round."

## II.—THE LIMITS WITHIN WHICH THE QUESTION WILL BE ARGUED.

Miracles naturally strike men with astonishment; but what is there in them to win men to repentance? There is this: miracles are signs of the Divine presence and activity. They feelingly persuade men that the God of whom they too habitually conceive as distant and quiescent is near them and with them, that He is at work in their midst. And how shall men become conscious of the immediate presence of God without at the same moment becoming conscious of the sins which have alienated them from Him? And how shall any man become profoundly conscious of sin without also becoming profoundly sorry for it?

Miracles, then, are a great means of grace; they tend to bring, and they are designed to bring, men to repentance, and through repentance to life.

Now this great means of grace was vouchsafed, our Lord tells us, to the men of Capernaum, Bethsaida, and Chorazin, although it failed to produce its proper effect upon them; and it was denied to the men of Sodom, and Tyre and Sidon, although it would *not* have failed to produce its proper effect on them.

Could any words well quicken in us deeper perplexity and distress of spirit? They seem to charge the Divine Providence with a double blunder. What would have sufficed to save one set of men was withheld from them; it was granted to another set of men, whom it did not suffice to save! Why was this waste —this double waste? Why were the works of Christ not done in the streets of those cities which would have repented had they witnessed them, instead of being thrown away on men to whom, since they did not bring them to repentance, they only brought a severer judgment?

The usual answer to that question is true so far as it goes; but does it go far enough to relieve our minds of the perplexity and distress in which the question inevitably involves them? It is reasonable to believe that, since men can only live as they come to know God and yet cannot find Him out for themselves, He should come and dwell with them, that He should disclose Himself to those who were groping after Him, if haply they might find Him. It is equally reasonable to believe that, if He came, He would come but once, once for all; that He would not be for ever breaking through that veil of natural forces and sequences behind which He at once hides and reveals Himself; that He would not become incarnate in every race and in every generation, but that once, in the fulness of the times, He would manifest forth his glory. But if that fit and selected time fell when Chorazin, and Bethsaida, and Capernaum were full of busy life, obviously there was no room for a Divine advent in that earlier period in which Sodom, and Tyre and Sidon were filling up the cup of their iniquities. *They* could not see the mighty works of Christ, even though they would long ago have repented had they seen them.

So much we admit, or may admit; and yet, does the admission satisfy us? Is it just that a man's salvation should depend on the age, or on the moral conditions of the age, into which he is born, and which he has done nothing to determine? If, for example, the citizens of ancient Tyre *would* have been quickened to eternal life by the presence and works of Christ, are they never to see Him? are they to be damned for not having seen Him? If Socrates, and Plato, and Aristotle, if Cicero, and Marcus Aurelius, and Epictetus, would have fallen at the feet of the Son of Man, and joyfully have taken Him for their Master and Friend, are they never to hear the gracious words that proceeded out of his mouth? Are they to be damned for not having heard them? And if many a Hindoo would have been saved by that very Gospel to which we turn so cold and indifferent an ear, will that Gospel never be preached to them? will they be damned for not having received it? And if they are, shall we say, "It is just"?

Many do say so. They argue that every race and generation of men has light enough if only they will walk by it, even though the great Light should not have risen upon them. It may be doubted whether such an argument would carry much weight even with those who most insist on it, if they themselves had been born in one of the dark ages or dark places of the earth, instead of standing, as they assume, in the full blaze of the Sun of Righteousness. For those who are content with this argument are commonly those who defer most to the current opinions of their time and set; in all probability they would have remained whatever they were born—Jews or Mohammedans, Parsees or Buddhists, and would have been no truer to the light that was in them than they are now. That any man who thinks for himself, and ponders the facts of human life in a sympathetic heart, and is capable of coming to a conclusion for himself, should maintain that every man born into the world has an equal or even a fair chance of getting to heaven, nay, that he should affirm that vast myriads of men have had any chance at all, is simply incredible. There are multitudes here in England, among the neglected and criminal classes, who have never had any real opportunity of knowing God or Christ, or even the blessedness of a pure and honest life; and there are multitudes more from whom the Light of Life has been concealed by the superstition, or the bigotry, or the immorality of the very Church itself. And who that knows the moral and spiritual conditions of these English multitudes will venture to affirm that in ancient Sodom, when Abraham himself was but stumbling through the first rudiments of religion, men had such means of knowing and loving God that they deserved to be damned for their neglect of them?

The conclusion to which we are driven when we really consider those words is, as I said in my last Lecture, that if the men of Sodom would have repented at the ministry of Christ, then this germ of life must, under the rule of that kind just God who suffers no vital germ of goodness to be destroyed, have been long since developed; they must long ago have seen the works of Christ, and have been brought by them to that life of which He Himself pronounced them capable. But as this conclusion runs right in the teeth of more than one popular dogma, we must proceed to examine a little in detail the ground on which it rests.

These dogmas, which happily are losing force daily, and daily moving through a lessening circle, are,—that there is no probation beyond the grave, that when men leave this world their fate is fixed beyond all hope of change; that if, when they die, they have not repented of their sins, so far from finding any place of repentance open to them in the life to come, they will be condemned to an eternal torment, or, at best, to a destructive torment which will annihilate them. And as these dogmas claim to be formulated interpretations of Scripture, it would be of little avail to shew that they are contrary to reason, that they offend against the plainest dictates of justice, that they distort and debase the very character of God. The appeal is to the Bible as the supreme authority.—as the only clear and indubitable revelation of the will of God; and to the Bible we must therefore go for any satisfactory and authoritative refutation of them. I, for one, however, cannot take this course without entering my protest against the assumption that Reason and Conscience are to have no voice in the determination of this, or of any other, theological question. Doubtless we hear the voice of God in Scripture, and in Scripture hear it most distinctly; but that voice also speaks within us, in our reason and in our moral sense. And he who has drawn a conclusion from Scripture which Reason and Conscience imperatively condemn should need no other proof that he has misinterpreted the Word of God. Still, as the appeal is to the Bible, we will go to the Bible, reserving our right, however, of interpreting it by our reason and conscience.

But here, at the very outset, the question presents itself: To what parts of the Bible may we fairly look for clear and authoritative teaching on the secrets or mysteries of the life to come? And obviously, if we know anything of the structure, history, and design of this great collection of Scriptures, we shall not for a moment assume that every book of the Bible speaks on all themes with equal distinctness and authority; that, wherever we find words that will serve our turn, we may detach them from their context, and attribute as much weight to them as though they fell from the lips of our Lord and his apostles. On the contrary, in selecting those Scriptures which will really aid us in our search, we shall have to lay aside by far the larger part of the Bible, not that we may induce it to speak our thought, but simply that we may argue the question fairly. The Old Testament, for example, except in so far as we can find large general principles in it which bear on our question, will be of no avail to us; for it is as certainly true as any such wide proposition can be, that the psalmists and prophets of old time never got more than momentary and partial glimpses of the life to come. We are expressly told that Christ "brought life and immortality to light;" and if that be true, clearly "life and immortality" were more or less hidden in darkness before He came: and we must not go to the darkness for light.

But if, for our present purpose, we must lay aside the Old Testament, it is equally obvious that we must also lay aside the last book of the New Testament, though for a very different reason. Possibly the Apocalypse would throw a clearer light on the mysteries of the life to come than any other Scripture, if only we had the key to it and could read it "with the understanding." But, confessedly, we have not the key to it; it is variously interpreted, interpreted on principles wholly incompatible with each other, by the most learned and devout students of the Bible, the best scholars, the soundest divines; and till some certain interpretation of it is reached, or at least some interpretation of it which shall command a wide and general assent, it would be unwise and unsafe for us to build any conclusion on our private interpretation of it.

These are very large deductions to be made—the whole Old Testament on the one hand, and on the other the Book of the Revelation; but unless we are to "fall out by the way," to wrangle over disputed interpretations of doubtful Scriptures, I do not see how we can refuse to make them. If we cannot, we have only the Gospels and the Epistles left. Our field of research, if much more limited, is also much more manageable. But even from this limited field there remains one deduction to be made, or rather, perhaps, I should say, that over the entrance to this lessened field a certain "Beware" must be inscribed. Many of our Lord's most familiar allusions to the future conditions of men are couched in parables; and to say that the details of parables must not be insisted on, that we must be cautious how we use them lest we should be landed in false conclusions, is, after all, only to repeat a maxim on which all Commentators are agreed, although it is also the plain dictates of common sense—a quality for which Commentators get even less credit than they deserve. Let us bear in mind, then, that if the parables of Christ are to be used in this argument, they must be used with modesty and discretion, since parables are but pictures of truth, comparisons of things not in the world of sense with things which are in that world, and such comparisons seldom run on all fours.

And be sure of this—or why should you listen to me at all? or how could we hope to travel to any conclusion together in peace?—that in asking you to exclude these Scriptures from the list of authorities to which we make our common appeal, I am not trying covertly to bring the Bible round to my view, or indeed to any view whatever. The Scriptures which we thus exclude are at least as favourable to the view to which my study of the Word of God long since led me, as to the more common and accepted view. If any man thinks that the Old Testament teaches the irrevocable condemnation of the vast majority of men at the moment they pass out of our sight, for every text he can adduce from it in support of that view, I will undertake to produce another which asserts the universality of the Divine Redemption, and implies the salvation of all men.[1] And so with the Apocalypse, and so with the Parables. Indeed, no one who has not given many years to the study of the Bible can so much as imagine how numerous and weighty are the passages, even in these excluded portions of the Inspired Volume, in favour of the conclusion that human life beyond the separating line of death is as varied, as flexible, as capable of change as it is on this side; and how many intimations they contain of the ultimate restitution of all souls. The fact is, that throughout the Bible there are two main lines of thought on this subject, though hitherto the Church has been too apt to recognize only one of them. The first affirms or implies that to sin, to be in sins, is to be damned both in this and in all other worlds; that so long as men are shut up in sin the wrath of God abides, and must abide, on them, whatever the sphere in which

[1] Some of these passages are cited in Lecture viii.

they move; that the only way to escape damnation, whether in this or in any other world, is to turn from sin, to come out of it, to exchange the "death in sin" for the "life in righteousness:" while the other line of thought affirms or implies that the wrath of God, the condemnation of sin, the punishments which are the natural and inevitable consequences of unrighteousness, are designed to correct men, to convict them of sin, to make them hate it and abandon it, that they may love righteousness and pursue it.

For the present, however, I must not dwell on this point; we shall recur to it again further on: but take just one illustration of it. You know what use has been made of such parables as those of Dives and Lazarus, the Wise and Foolish Virgins, the Sheep and the Goats. You know, too, how those who lay great stress on such details of these parables as "the great gulf," the shut door, the left and the right hand of the Judge—as if the left hand were not the next best place to the right hand, or a door once shut could never again be opened, or a gulf once impassable could never be bridged: you know, I say, how apt those who lay stress on such points would be to suspect that the Parables were excluded from our field of view because they told against the conclusion to which I am trying to lead you. But do they tell against it? Suppose we also cared to violate an accepted canon of criticism by laying stress on the details of parables, what bright and happy inferences might we not draw from such parables as these? "The kingdom of heaven is like unto leaven, which a woman took and hid in three measures of meal, till *the whole* was leavened;" or again, "What man of you, having a hundred sheep, if he lose one of them, doth not leave the ninety and nine in the wilderness, and go after that which is lost *until he find it?*" Would it not be quite easy to interpret these weighty and emphatic phrases as signifying that the whole mass of mankind is to be leavened and quickened by the truth of Christ, and that the great Bishop of our souls will never cease from his quest of any poor lost sinner until he find him and restore him to the fold? Might we not even insist on reading that "pearl of parables," the Prodigal Son, in a very novel and surprising light? Might we not take the righteous, and self-righteous, brother as a type of those good people who, with Luther, think it "the highest degree of faith to believe that God is merciful who saves so few and damns so many," and imagine, with St Thomas Aquinas, that in the world to come their bliss "may please them the more because they are permitted to gaze on the punishment of the wicked"? Might we not take the younger son as a type of those whom *they* call "the lost," and the "far country" as hell, and the return to the Father as the recovery of the self-doomed sinner from the error of his ways? It is very certain that in so reading these parables we should depart no farther from the dictates of common sense and the canons of sound criticism than do those who pile up so great a weight of dogma on similar phrases and analogies in other parables.

But if in answer to the question, To what parts of the Bible may we look for clear and authentic light on the mysteries of the life to come? we have determined to confine ourselves to the plain teaching of our Lord and his apostles, *i.e.*, to the very cream of Scripture; if we have gone so far as to select our materials, another question forthwith meets us, viz., What sort of structure may we hope to rear with them? May we hope to frame a clear, full, and coherent theory of the life that is both spiritual and eternal? to determine with precision what the fate, whether of the good or of the bad, will be when they put off the tabernacle of the flesh?

No reflective man will for a moment suppose that, while we are compassed about with the limits and crippling infirmities of the flesh, we can hope to comprehend what the purely spiritual life will be; or that in this, the first stage of our being, we are able so much as to conceive what the final stage of our course will be like. Christ descended into Hades; yet when He came back to earth He disclosed none of the secrets of the prison-house. Paul was caught up into Paradise, and saw some faint shadow of its glory; yet he maintained to the last that it was impossible for him to utter what he had seen and heard, albeit he was a great master of the most subtle and flexible language spoken among men. And a little reflection will convince us that that which is eternal cannot be fairly, or, if fairly, cannot be fully, comprehended by those whose thoughts are governed and conditioned by the sequences of time; that so long as we are to be approached from without only through avenues of sense, that which is purely spiritual can only be set before us in pictures, in similitudes and analogies, which, like all analogies and comparisons, have their inevitable defects, and conceal almost as much as they disclose, in some cases even more. All deep knowledge presupposes not only the proper faculties for acquiring it, but that those faculties should have been highly trained and developed. It is of no use to talk the higher mathematics, to pick holes, for instance, in the differential calculus, as our friend James Hinton was so fond of doing, to one who has not even mastered the elements of arithmetic and geometry.

Nay, a knowledge beyond our reach may be simply injurious and misleading to us. We know very well, for example, that we should only injure young children were we to discuss with them some of the commonest facts of our own mature life, that we should awaken a morbid and prurient curiosity in them, and that our words would only mislead them because they would take other shapes and relations, quicken other trains of association in their minds, to those which they assume and quicken in our own. In short, we are aware that by trying to communicate a knowledge for which they are necessarily unprepared, we should simply impose an intolerable and degrading burden on them. How is it then that we do not see, if indeed we do not, that we ourselves are too immature and untrained to grasp the mysteries of eternity, of an absolute and unconditioned existence, or of an existence whose conditions are utterly different from our own? We ought to be aware, when we reflect upon it we are aware, that if, while we are still babes in the spiritual life, clothed with flesh, conditioned by time, the secrets of the unclothed, unconditioned, spiritual world could be put into any words with which we are familiar, they would only mislead and oppress us. What faith can apprehend and realize, what the intuitions of love can grasp, this indeed lies open to us, and is helpful to us, as we see in the case of children; but the points with which speculation would busy itself and a merely intellectual curiosity, these are mercifully hidden from our eyes.

What, then, *may* we hope to learn from these

selected Scriptures concerning the life to come ? We may hope, I think, to see, on the one hand, that the Scriptures, when fairly interpreted, do not sustain that theory of the future state which has long found general acceptance, and which, like so much else in the Roman Church—from which we have derived it—seems to be a survival of ancient heathen beliefs shewing through the thin Christian varnish with which Papal theologians have sought to disguise it; and, on the other hand, we may hope to find that there are great principles, principles that run through the Bible from end to end, which point conclusively to a very different theory—a theory consistent at once with our highest conceptions of the character of God and with the dictates of reason and conscience. In fine, I would advise any of you who wish to know what the Bible really teaches of the future life, first, to study attentively all those passages in the Gospels and Epistles which are commonly adduced in favour of the endless punishment of the impenitent, for you will find that they are at least patient of another than the current interpretation; and then, refusing to pin your faith to any theory built on isolated texts and passages, to inquire what large, general, pervading truths, what spacious and controlling principles, are woven into the very stuff and substance of Scripture which bear on this question, and what are the conclusions to which they point.

That surely is the reasonable method to pursue; and if you care to pursue it, I will try in my succeeding Lectures to shew you how to use it and to what conclusion it leads.

## III.—DAMNATION.

In the two previous and preliminary Lectures we have arrived at the following conclusions :—

(1.) That we must look for what the Bible has to teach on the life to come only to the Gospels and the Epistles, since the Old Testament Scriptures were written before life and immortality had been brought to light, while the Apocalypse is written in a cipher of which we do not possess the key.

(2.) That, even with the Gospels and Epistles in our hands, we must not hope to frame a full, exact, and coherent theory of that life, since it is by no means likely that the sacred and august realities of the spiritual and eternal world can be revealed to us with any fulness and precision so long as we are the children of sense and time.

(3.) But that we may hope, by a patient study of the passages commonly adduced in favour of the endless punishment of the impenitent,—($\alpha$) to shew that they do not sustain the interpretation put upon them; and ($\beta$) to find in these Scriptures, nay, in the whole Bible, certain large and controlling principles which point in an entirely opposite direction.

So that what we have yet to do is to examine the texts which seem to imply that, when the wicked die out of this world, there is no longer any prospect of their being recovered unto life, since they are instantly damned to an interminable and unremedial torment; and then to look for those great ruling principles which render any such conclusion impossible.

I need hardly say, I suppose, that of those two branches of inquiry the second is by far the more attractive and conclusive. To build up a doctrine on isolated texts is always hazardous and unsatisfactory. Before we can rely on our doctrine we must assure ourselves that it is in harmony with the ruling thoughts which pervade the Scripture from end to end, that it accords with the mind of the Spirit rather than with the letter of the Word. But, on the other hand, it would be of little use to discuss these large ruling thoughts or principles, and to draw logical conclusions from them, if, all the while we were thus occupied, we were fretted and harassed by the recollection of a considerable number of passages which *would* perk up their heads and open their lips to question, if not to contradict, the conclusions to which we were travelling. We must, therefore, clear these passages out of our way, must determine what they really teach, if we are to frame our conclusion with an undisturbed mind, and to rest in it. To this task, then, a careful and honest examination of the Scriptures which favour, or appear to favour, the accepted view, let us at once address ourselves.

Now, if we ask on what, and what kind of passages in the Gospels and Epistles the popular view is based, I think we shall find that they are of two classes. (1) We have all those passages in which the words "hell" and "damnation" occur; then (2) we have a still larger class, in which the words "eternal" and "everlasting" occur; and in this class, a subordinate series in which precisely the same epithets are applied to the reward of the good and the punishment of the wicked, from which therefore the inference is drawn that the one will endure as long as the other. Under these two heads we may gather up, I think, all that is of real value and importance in the New Testament, in so far, at least, as it bears on the question we have in hand. To examine these passages at all carefully, or even to examine the leading examples of each class, is a work that will necessarily consume some time; but I hope three or four Lectures will suffice to take us through them; and then we shall be free to turn to the study of those spacious and controlling principles by which, after all, the question must be finally determined.

The first class of Scriptures we have to examine are those in which the words "*hell*" and "*damnation*" occur, for it is on these passages mainly that the popular misconception is based. If these two words were expunged from the Bible, I doubt whether most of those who read it would not feel that the whole dogma of future and endless torment had vanished with them. No doubt, therefore, many of you will be surprised—perhaps even astonished and indignant—to hear, that *neither of these words is to be found in any part of the New Testament*, or, indeed, in any part of the whole Bible; nor even any word which at all answers to the conception which they quicken in our minds. "Not to be found in the New Testament!" you say; "why I can shew you a dozen, or a score of places in which these words are to be found." But are you quite sure that it is the New Testament in which you find them? It is a version, a translation of the New Testament, of course; but does it necessarily follow that the translation is an accurate one? I am sorry to say, that in so far as it uses the words "hell" and "damnation," it is demonstrably an inaccurate and misleading one. No such words are to be found in the Greek, that is, in the real, the original Testament, nor any words which convey, as *they* now do, the conception of a final and ever-during place of torment, and of a Divine sentence which adjudges men to that place of torment.

Now, as that is a very grave assertion to make, as it must seem so strange to many of you as to be almost incredible, I must proceed to prove and vindicate it in some detail. And as no proof would be quite satisfactory to you that did not explain how words have crept into our Authorized Version which are not to be found in the Greek Original, let me show you how our translators came to employ the words damnation and hell. *They* are not to blame, or not much to blame. Their own minds were tinctured, imbued, with the mediæval theology of the Roman Church, which Church, as you know, had greatly erred from "the simplicity that is in Christ." And, moreover, they were strictly charged to "retain the old ecclesiastical words," so far as possible, and to employ them in the sense in which they had been commonly used by the doctors of that Church. And still further, neither of these words had then quite stiffened and narrowed into the sense in which it is now understood. The word "hell" comes from an old English or Teutonic word, *hel-an*, which means " to cover," and, in the ancient use of it, it signified any covered place. In our early English literature it is used of any obscure dungeon or covered spot, even of the dark hole into which a tailor threw his shreds and clippings; nay, even of the retired and bosky shade to which the lads and lasses caught in a game called *Barley-break* were led to pay the forfeit of a kiss. And, in like manner, the verb "to damn" probably came from an old Teutonic verb, "*deman*," to deem. It is at least closely related to the words "deem" and "doom." It meant *to deem* any one guilty of any kind of offence, and *to doom* him to its appropriate punishment. Thus, for example, a man might be *damned* to prison, *i.e.*, *deemed* worthy of it, and *doomed* to it; or his goods might be *damnified*, *i.e.*, injured or *condemned*; or a play might be *damned*, *i.e.*, hissed off the stage, *deemed* too poor for farther representation, and *doomed* never to appear again.

Both these words, therefore, were innocent enough in themselves originally, and had many harmless uses. But Theology has put meanings into them which make them the most terrible words in our language; and for many years now they have been used almost exclusively in a theological sense. When *we* meet the word "hell," it conveys no innocent and cheerful suggestions. In many minds it quickens only an image of some vast and burning prison, in which lost souls writhe and shriek for ever, tormented in a flame that will never be quenched. To those who reject the conception of a vast material hell, an endless physical torture, the word suggests a place or condition in which the souls of the wicked, kept in life for that end by the mighty power of God, are for ever consumed by pangs compared with which the horrors of a furnace would be a paradise. To be *damned* is, at least for us, to be adjudged to that intolerable torment, without any hope of amendment or release. The meaning of these words, therefore, has greatly and horribly changed; and whatever excuse we may make for the use of them by King James's translators, there is no shadow of excuse for those who now use them to translate the New Testament Greek.

That you may be convinced of this, let us examine the passages in which they occur. Take the verb "*to damn*," first. The word is so frequent in the mouth of Theology that it is with some surprise we ascertain that it only occurs twelve times in the New Testament; that in some of these cases it cannot possibly have the sense we put upon it: and that in no single instance is any equivalent word employed in the Original. Before we turn to these passages, and in order that you may understand them, let me give those of you who need it a little lesson in Greek. It shall be a very short and simple one, and any of you may master it in a minute or two. In the Greek, one of the verbs in the most common use is κρίνειν (*krinein*). Any Lexicon will tell you that κρίνειν means "to part, to separate, to discriminate between good and bad," in short, "to judge." From this verb, κρίνειν, two nouns are formed, κρίσις (*krisis*), which means the act of deciding or judging, and κρίμα (*krima*), which means the sentence, or judgment, which has been reached. From this verb, κρίνειν, moreover, another verb has been formed by prefixing a preposition to it, which intensifies its meaning, viz., κατα-κρίνειν (*kata-krinein*), "to give judgment *against*, to condemn." And from this second verb, as from the first, two nouns are formed—κατά-κρισις (*kata-krisis*), the act of condemning, and κατά-κριμα (*kata-krima*), "the sentence of condemnation." All you need remember is, that in the Greek there is a verb, κρίνειν, which, with its derivatives, means "to judge," "the act of judging," and "the sentence of justice;" and another verb, κατα-κρίνειν, which, with its derivatives, means "to condemn," "the act of condemning," and "the sentence of condemnation." There are hardly any words in the Greek language more common than these; and there is not, and never has been, any dispute as to their meaning.

Now the former of these two verbs, κρίνειν, with its derivatives, occurs more than a hundred and seventy times in the Greek Testament; more than a hundred and fifty times it is rendered in the English Version by our verb "to judge," so that our translators evidently knew its plain meaning and use. Seven times, very needlessly and misleadingly, it is rendered by "to condemn;" twice by "to accuse"; and only eight times by "to damn." That is to say, our own translators render the word in the sense of to damn, *only eight times out of nearly a hundred and eighty!* So, again, with the other Greek verb, κατα-κρίνειν, which means to condemn. With its derivatives it is used twenty-four times in the New Testament, and only twice do they render it by "to damn;" in every other instance they abide by its true meaning—"to condemn."

You see how the case stands then. These two Greek verbs occur some two hundred times in the New Testament, and in only ten instances is this dreadful, this *damnable*, meaning foisted upon them! Is there anything in the intention and contexture of these ten passages to warrant so grave a departure from the common and admitted meanings of the words? Look at them for yourselves, and see.

Turn to St Mark xii. 40. Our Lord is warning his hearers against the Scribes who "devour widows' houses, and for a pretence make long prayers." "These," He adds, according to our Authorized Translation at least, "shall receive *greater damnation*." The Greek says simply, "These shall receive *the severer judgment*." And the plain meaning of the passage is, that the very hypocrisy under which the Scribes thought to cloak their crimes would only bring a heavier *krima*, or verdict, upon them. Both good men and God would pass the sharper sentence on them for the semblance of piety behind which they veiled their impious and insatiable greed. It is a general truth which Christ here enunciates, a truth as applicable and as pertinent to the present life as to any other. It has no special bearing on the future life until we import that bearing into it by substituting the word "damnation" for the word "judgment." To warn men in general terms that, if they add the sin of hypocrisy to the sin of extortion, they will inevitably expose themselves to a keener censure, is one thing; but surely it is another and a very different thing to threaten them with being shut up in an interminable hell the very moment they die!

If any think that even to restore the true word "judgment" in this and similar passages makes very little difference in their meaning; if they take the "judgment" of God as equivalent to "damnation," that can only be because they conceive of the Divine judgments as though they were confined to the future life, whereas the Scriptures constantly affirm that God judges all men, good and bad, every day and all day long; and because they wholly misapprehend the character of the Divine Judge and Father. A man who is a magistrate judges many men whom he does not condemn, whom mere justice, to say nothing of compassion, will not allow him to condemn; he condemns even most of those whom he finds guilty to a limited punishment which is intended for their correction: and what conception must *they* have formed of the Father of an infinite justice and mercy who assume that He will never judge men save to condemn them, and never condemn them to any punishment short of an illimitable and degrading agony?

St Matthew xxiii. 33. According to our English Version our Lord demands of the same wicked and unhappy class of men, the Scribes, "How shall ye escape *the damnation of hell?*" The full explanation of this passage I defer till we reach that other class of texts in which the word "hell" is employed. For the present I ask you to mark only that in the Greek we read simply, "How shall ye escape *the judgment,*" not the damnation, "of Gehenna?"

St Mark iii. 29. Our Lord is speaking of the sin against the Holy Ghost. He who commits that sin "can never be forgiven," or, literally, "cannot be forgiven in this age," and is "in danger of *eternal damnation.*" So, at least, the Authorized Version affirms. But even the Greek Text from which our Version was made, only affirms that such a sinner is in danger of "eternal *judgment;*" and that Text is now admitted to be corrupt, the true reading being, "eternal *sin.*" What our Lord meant by a man's coming into the grip of an æonial or eternal sin, we may inquire hereafter; all we now have to do is to discharge the word "damnation" from the passage; to affirm that it should never have been thrust into it, since the word before our translators only meant "judgment," and that

that word must now be replaced by one which means "sin."

St John v. 29. Our Lord affirms that all who are in their graves shall one day hear his voice and come forth, "they that have done good to the resurrection of life, and they that have done evil to the resurrection of *damnation*." Here again the word is *krisis*, and the phrase should read, "they that have done evil to the resurrection of *judgment*."

Romans iii. 8. The Apostle Paul, speaking of men who made it their maxim, "Let us do evil that good may come," affirms that "their *damnation* is just." The Greek word is *krima*, and means *judgment;* and I take the holy Apostle to assert that the instinctive verdict of the human heart against those who act on that detestable maxim is a true, a just, verdict. There is no reference whatever, or at least no necessary reference, either to the judgment of God or to the recompenses of a future state.

In Romans xiii. 2, the same Apostle is enforcing obedience to the public authorities. He asserts that there is no "power" which is not ordained of God; that to resist any such power is therefore to resist God's ordinance: and he adds, "they that resist shall receive to themselves *damnation*." Once more the word is *krima;* and the sentence means simply that those who resist the public authorities will expose themselves to *judgment, i.e.,* to the censure of their contemporaries, of the authorities, and perhaps also of God Himself. We too much forget that we all have and shall have, to answer at the bar of God for all we do,—for our thoughts as well as for our words, for our motives as well as for our actions. And no doubt the more momentous and influential our thoughts, or words, or actions are, the more strict and searching will be the account to which we shall be called, both in this age and in the next, and in the next to that, and in all the ages through which we pass. And if St Paul intended any reference to the judgment of God here, he intended to warn men that even those who lead a revolt against an intolerable and degrading despotism will have to answer for it to God ; that a special and heavy responsibility rests on those who stir up men's hearts to sudden mutiny, to a desperate resistance of even the most abused public authority. That is very wholesome doctrine, whether St Paul intended to teach it or not. Men *should* weigh well what they do when they think to follow in the steps of the great patriots and martyrs. Rebellion, like matrimony, " is not by any to be enterprised, nor taken in hand unadvisedly, lightly or wantonly, but reverently, advisedly, soberly, and in the fear of God." But can any sane man take the words of St Paul to mean that the patriots who won the freedom of ancient Greece or Rome, or of modern England and America, by resisting the powers set over them, have been *damned* for resisting them? Yet that, you see, is what our Authorized Version affirms or implies; so that, in this case at least, mere common sense teaches us that it must be faulty and misleading.

There is another and a somewhat similar instance in that very curious passage, 1 Timothy v. 12. It would seem that in some of the Apostolic Churches there arose a class of women devoted to a single life, who gave themselves to works of hospitality and mercy. Their names were entered on an official roll. And on this roll Timothy was advised not to enter the names of any young widows, nor indeed of any woman under sixty years of age, lest the younger women should repent of their vows. "They will marry again," says St Paul, " having *damnation*, because they have cast off their first faith." Is it, then, so great a crime for a young widow, even though she has vowed she would never marry again, to contract a second marriage, that she must needs be damned for it? What more, or worse, could befall her had she violated every commandment in the Decalogue? Is a sister of mercy, or a nun—such an one as Luther's wife, for example—to be adjudged to an everlasting torment, should she swerve from her single estate? Surely not; for once more the Greek word is *krima*, and means no more than "judgment." Such a woman will not be *damned* for breaking her vow; but, if she have taken that vow rashly and heedlessly and then should break it, she will very certainly be *judged*, perhaps severely judged, not by God alone, but also by men, and, above all, by women. Vows are too solemn to be lightly taken or lightly broken, whether they be vows of marriage or vows against marriage; and therefore Timothy is not to let those take them who are only too likely to break them.

The two passages we have just considered are instances of the absurd, almost grotesque, way in which this word "damnation" has been thrust into our Version of the New Testament, without any warrant from the Original, and in the teeth both of common sense and common humanity. But, nevertheless, you must remember what use has been made of this absurd blunder by that priestly caste which has too long dominated and degraded the Church. Planting themselves on this blunder, they have solemnly pronounced *all* rebellion against kings and governors, even when provoked by the most intolerable despotism, to be an inexpiable crime, and have exulted in the certain damnation of such noble patriots as Hampden, Cromwell, Milton, Washington, Cavour; they have also pronounced any and every violation even of the most senseless vows to be a crime not to be forgiven whether in this world or in the world to come : and thus, century after century, a blunder for which a school-boy would be whipped has been used by them to narrow the thoughts of men, to dull their consciences, and to inflict an agony of doubt and shame on many sensitive hearts which we can hardly so much as conceive.

But even these are not the most cruel results of this fatal inaccuracy. There is one passage which, as it stands in our Authorized Version, has darkened and pierced with pangs of deadly fear myriads of tender consciences, very mainly because the word "damnation" is substituted in it for the word "judgment." In 1 Corinthians xi. 29 we read, "He that eateth and drinketh unworthily, eateth and drinketh *damnation* to himself, not discerning the Lord's body," although here again the Greek word is *krima*, *i.e.*, *judgment*. And thus the gracious assurance that even if we come to the table of the Lord in a spirit unworthy of that sacred mystery, because we have not first judged ourselves, we shall be judged, judged here and now, in order that we may not be condemned with the world (vers. 31 and 32), is converted into a horrible menace, which has kept thousands from the communion of the body and blood of Christ, that we shall be damned to an everlasting loss and ruin !

In 2 Thessalonians ii. 12 St Paul refers to some who would not receive the truth, and predicts that

God will suffer them to be deluded by lies, in order that "they all might be *damned* who believed not the truth, but had pleasure in unrighteousness." But here too the verb is *krinein,* and all that St Paul says is that they will be *judged,* without so much as hinting what the judgment may be or when it will take place.

These are all the instances in which the verb *krinein* ("to judge") is rendered in our Version by the English verb "to damn." But there are two passages in which that other verb (*katakrinein*), which means *to condemn,* is thus rendered. The first is St Mark xvi. 16 (a verse not contained however in the most ancient MSS.), "He that believeth not shall be *damned,*" where the rendering should be, "He that believeth not shall be *condemned.*" And the second, Romans xiv. 23, "He that doubteth is *damned* if he eat," where of course we ought to read, "He that hath scruples is, if he eat, *condemned*"—condemned, *i.e.,* by his own conscience for doing what that conscience disallows. The notion that the weak brother who thinks it wrong, or thinks that it may be wrong, to eat of meat offered to idols will be doomed to hell for eating them, is utterly and grossly alien to the Apostle's mind. No one would have been more shocked by such an extravagance than he.

There are still two instances in which the word is used in our Translation; but in these the mistake is acknowledged by all students of the Bible. They both occur in 2 Peter ii. 1-3, where the Apostle speaks of those who bring in "*damnable* heresies," and says of them "whose *damnation* slumbereth not." Here a new word is used in the Greek, a word we have not met before, and the meaning of which we need not discuss, since it is admitted on all hands that the Greek should be rendered "*destructive* heresies," heresies destructive to the Faith, and "whose *destruction* slumbereth not." What the Apostle means is evidently that those who introduce destructive heresies shall themselves be destroyed by them; but how, and when, and where, he deponeth not.

I have now cited every passage in which the verb "to damn," in any form of it, is used in our Version. And, as you see, in no single case is there, in the Original, the slightest warrant for its use. With a clear conscience, therefore, and a thankful heart, we may discharge this horrible word from the pages of the New Testament. It should never have been permitted to defile them. There is no shadow of excuse for retaining it when once we have learned that the Greek words it is employed to render never mean more than to judge and to condemn. We are all of us judged by God every day that we live, and often condemned. And we shall all be judged by Him when we die, and even then some of us may be condemned.

But to what we shall be condemned none of the passages we have yet examined declare. And, therefore, we have no right to import into them, as we do by our present translation, the notion that we shall be doomed to an endless torment, or even to the final and irrevocable loss of hope.

In my next Lecture I will try to shew you that we may send the word "hell" after the word "damnation," and for ever have done with them both.

## IV.—HELL.

IN my last Lecture I shewed you what I hope you found to be good and conclusive reasons for expunging the verb "to damn," with its derivatives, from our translation of the Bible; and I am now to shew you, if I can, equally good and conclusive reasons for expunging the word "hell."

This word comes, as I have said, from an old English or Teutonic word, *hel-an*, and means any covered place. In our early literature it is used to denote, not only any obscure place or dungeon, but also the dark hole into which a tailor flung his waste shreds, and even the retired spot to which, in a popular game, a lad led a lass to exact the forfeit of a kiss. But Theology has long since discharged all gay and innocent meanings and associations from the word "hell." It only calls up in our minds either some faint image of a vast prison or furnace, in which the impenitent are tormented in a flame that will never be quenched; or of a vast and awful realm in which their spirits are to be searched through and through with intolerable and never-ending pangs. In short, those who hold the orthodox, or hyper-orthodox, dogma maintain that at death, or at latest after the resurrection, the wicked will be turned into a place of torment, torment physical or meta-physical, torment uncorrective and therefore without an end.

Now in this theological sense, the sense in which we naturally take the word when we meet it in the Bible, I am bold to say that the word "hell" is never once used in the Original, though it is so frequent in our translation of it, and that we have no longer any sort of excuse for retaining it on the sacred page. There is no word at all answering to it whether in the Hebrew or in the Greek. *We*, however, are not concerned with the whole Bible; we have agreed to confine our search for light on the future conditions of men to the Gospels and the Epistles. In our Authorized Version of *these* Scriptures, then, the word "hell" occurs eighteen times, and is used to render the three Greek words, *Tartarus*, *Hades*, and *Gehenna;* at each of which we will look in turn.

1. The word *Tartarus* occurs but once in the whole New Testament, or, indeed, in the whole Bible. You will find the passage in 2 Peter ii. 4, and a very singular passage it is. The holy Apostle is arguing that the Lord knows how "to reserve unrighteous men, under punishment, *unto the day of judgment.*" He is not speaking, therefore, of the *final* estate of the unrighteous, but of the state in which they are to await that great and terrible day. To prove his point,

he refers to the punishments which turned Sodom and Gomorrha into ashes, and swept away Noah's ungodly generation with a flood. But the first example to which he appeals is that of the doom which fell on the angels who kept not their first estate. His words are: " God spared not angels who sinned, but *cast them into Tartarus,* delivering them over into dens of darkness, to be held in custody unto"—with a view to—" judgment." Now it is very curious that St Peter, a simple and unlettered man, should have used this word " Tartarus," a word never occurring elsewhere in the Bible, not even in the writings of St Paul, the most learned of the Apostles. One can hardly help asking, with an accent of wonder, where he got it from, and how he came to use it; for it is a purely heathen word, and embodies a purely heathen conception. As they pryed into the future the Greeks and Romans saw nothing clearly, although " the initiated," perhaps, had been quickened into an intense yearning for, if not a bright and vivid hope of a life to come. The world beyond the gates of death was, for them, " a world of shades." Their utmost hope even for the good was that some thin shadow of the former man would survive, to enjoy some faint shadow of his former honours and pursuits. The utmost they foreboded for the wicked was that their thin, wavering, unsubstantial ghosts would be doomed to hopeless tasks, or consumed by pangs such as men suffer here. Sometimes they gave the name Tartarus to the whole of this land of shadows; but more commonly they divided the underworld into two provinces—the Elysian fields, in which the spirits of their heroes and their sages, with all who loved goodness, wandered to and fro, illumined by a pale reflection of their former joys; reserving the name Tartarus for that dismal region in which the ghosts of the wicked were tasked, and tantalized, and tormented.[1]

*Here,* no doubt, St Peter uses it in its more limited sense, and means to imply that the angels who sinned were cast into that gloomier province of the under-

---

[1] Mr Mahaffy, one of the ablest and best-read of our modern classical scholars, has some remarks on this point, which illustrate and confirm both what I have here said on the pagan conception of the Tartarean world, and what I have yet to say on the ancient conception of Hades. "We know from Homer and from Mimnermus, that in the earliest periods, though the Greeks were unable to shake off a belief in life after death, yet they could not conceive that state as anything but a shadowy and wretched echo of the real life upon earth. It was a gloomy and dark existence, burdened with the memory of lost happiness and the longing for lost enjoyment. To the Homeric Greeks their death was a dark unavoidable fate, without hope and without reward. It is, indeed, true that we find in Pindar thoughts and aspirations of a very different kind. We have in the fragments of his poetry which remain to us more than one passage asserting the reward of the just, and the splendours of a future life far happier than that which we now enjoy. But, notwithstanding these splendid visions, such high expectation laid no hold upon the imagination of the Greek world. The poems of Pindar, we are told, soon ceased to be popular, and his utterances are but a streak of light amid general gloom. The kingdom of the dead in Æschylus is evidently, as in Homer, but a weary echo of this life, where honour can only be attained by the pious memory of attached relations;

world which was the haunt of the wicked. Probably the Apostle did not know, nor affect to know, *much* of the angels who sinned and fell, and of what became of them after their fall. Probably it was because their fate was dim and shadowy to him that he employed a word, Tartarus, which carried only a dim and shadowy significance. But very certainly his " Tartarus " by no means answered to our " Hell." He was speaking, not of the final estate, whether of sinful men or of sinful angels, but of a state in which they are held *until the day of judgment arrives.* The word Tartarus would call up in the minds of his readers only

where duty paid to the dead affects him in his gloomier state, and raises him in the esteem of his less-remembered fellows. Sophocles says nothing to clear away the night; nay, rather his last and maturest contemplation regards death as the worst of ills to the happy man—a sorry refuge to the miserable. Euripides longs that there may be no future state, and Plato only secures the immortality of the soul by severing it from the person, the man, and all his interests."—(*Rambles and Studies in Greece*, pp. 69, 70.) In the same work (pp. 153-56) he develops the hint I have given above, that perhaps "the initiated" had been taught to "faintly trust the larger hope." Cicero (*De Legg*, ii. 14, § 36) has a memorable passage on the *Mysteries*: "Much that is excellent and divine does Athens seem to me to have produced and added to our life, but nothing better than those *Mysteries*, by which we are formed and moulded from a rude and savage life to humanity; and indeed in the *Mysteries* we perceive the real principles of life, and *learn*, not only to live happily, but *to die with a fairer hope.*" Commenting on this passage Mr Mahaffy asks what it was that gave these celebrated Mysteries, the greater Eleusinia, so transcendant a character that all the greatest minds of Greece and Rome speak of them with enthusiasm. And his reply is: "There is only one reasonable cause, and it is that which all our serious authorities agree upon—the doctrine taught in the most vague and undefined conceptions of some intermediate state. And, therefore, we have no right to translate it by a word which we use to denote the final state, the last and unchangeable lot of guilty men, and which calls up in our minds the most definite and terrible conceptions. Our plain duty to the passage is to read it in English as it reads in the original Greek, "God spared not angels who sinned, but cast them into *Tartarus.*"

2. The word *Hades* occurs five times in the Gospels and Epistles; and in every instance our translators render it by the word "hell." That the translation is

the Mysteries was a faith which revealed to them hopeful things about the world to come, and which, not so much as a condition, but as a consequence of this clearer light, this higher faith, made them better citizens and better men. This faith was taught them in the Mysteries through symbols, through prayer and fasting, through wild rejoicings; but, as Aristotle expressly tells us, it was reached, not by intellectual persuasion, but by a change into a new moral state—in fact, by being spiritually revived." After adverting to the wonderful fidelity with which this secret, known to so many, has been kept, so that we have nothing but hints of the "scenes of darkness and fear in which the hopeless state of the unbelievers was pourtrayed, and of light and glory to which the convert attained, when at last his eyes were opened to the knowledge of good and evil," he sums up thus: "But all these things are fragmentary glimpses, as are also the doctrines hinted of the unity of God, and of atonement by sacrifice. There remains nothing clear and certain but the unanimous verdict as to the greatness, the majesty, and the awe of the services, and as to the great spiritual knowledge and comfort which they conveyed. The consciousness of guilt was not, indeed, first taught by them, but was felt generally, and felt very keenly, by the Greek mind. These Mysteries were its Gospel of Reconciliation with the offended gods."

an inaccurate one, and at times even a grotesquely inaccurate one, it will be easy to shew.

The word *Hades* (ἀϊδές, from α = not, and ιδεῖν = to see) means, according to its derivation, that which is not and cannot be seen. According to its usage, it denotes in especial that vast subterranean kingdom, that dim shadow-world, into which the spirits of all men, good and bad alike, were held to pass at death. When they die, *men* are no longer seen; they pass over into the land which, if not dark in itself, is dark to us, hidden behind impenetrable veils of mystery. This, at least, was a common, perhaps the most common, conception of the future state among both the Eastern and Western nations of antiquity,[1] most of whom assumed the earth to be a vast plain, floating through space as "a broad leaf floats through air," the upper side of which, illumined by the sun, was reserved for the living, while the spirits of the dead were condemned to the dark under-surface, *i.e.*, to what we should call "the Antipodes." And the Jews shared, or adopted, this conception. They, too, thought of the kingdom of the dead as a vast under-world, in which the disembodied spirits of men would dwell until the day of judgment. In this vast kingdom there were two provinces, separated from each other

---

See Dr Draper's "History of the Intellectual Development of Europe," vol. i., *passim*.

by an impassable gulf—*Paradise,* answering to the Elysian fields of the heathen poets, and *Gehenna,* answering to their Tartarus. In Paradise the souls of the righteous awaited their final and complete blessedness; while in Gehenna the souls of the wicked awaited their final doom. To this entire kingdom, including both provinces, they gave the name *Hades.* For them Hades included Paradise as well as Gehenna; and therefore it is obviously inaccurate and misleading to render the word Hades, as our translators do, by the word "hell." Nay, the word "hell" is in *every* case a false and misleading rendering of the word Hades; for (1), Hades is never once used to denote the final estate of men, but only the state which precedes the day of judgment; and (2), it is commonly used to denote the whole of that intermediate state, the lot of the righteous as well as that of the unrighteous. Thus, for example, Josephus speaks of the spirit of Samuel as being evoked *from Hades* to warn King Saul of his approaching doom; and we may be very sure that Josephus did not conceive of that great prophet as doomed to an everlasting torment. Indeed, all the best ancient writers, Greek and Roman, Jewish and Christian, speak of their noblest men as dwelling in Hades, and looking with solemn expectation and sustaining hope for the dawn of some great day of deliverance. And the word is used in precisely the same sense both in the Gospels and in the Epistles.

Thus, in St Matthew xi. 23, we have our Lord's pathetic apostrophe: "And thou, Capernaum, which art exalted unto heaven, shalt be brought down to *Hades!*" So at least it stands in the Original, and not, as in our Version, "*to hell.*" And no doubt the thought in his mind was, that all that busy multitude of living men who then thronged the streets of Capernaum, would, ere long, be hurried into the dark under-world, leaving their favoured city desolate—as it is to this day.

In St Matthew xvi. 18, we have his gracious promise to Simon Barjona: "Thou art *Petros* (a rock), and on this *petra* (or rock), I will build my church; and the gates of *Hades* shall not prevail against it;" that is to say, no spiritual principalities and powers from the unseen world, whether bringing with them airs from Paradise or blasts from Gehenna, shall ever overthrow the Church animated by the spirit of that loyal and zealous Apostle. No thought of "hell," the final prison-house, was in our Lord's mind.

I have said that we must be careful not to push the details of any parable too far, that we must not go to parables for clear and authoritative teaching on the future conditions of the human race. But I gave you that caution simply because it is dictated both by common sense and by sound criticism, not because the Parables tell against my argument. They tell in favour of it, as you may see by referring to St Luke xvi. 23. In the parable of the Rich Man and Lazarus, our Lord describes the *after* condition of him who *here* was clothed in purple and fine linen, and fared sumptuously every day, thus: "And *in Hades* he lift up his eyes, being in torment." Here, of course, the word Hades stands for, or at least includes, that dark province of the under-world in which the unrighteous receive the due reward of their deeds; but is it therefore equivalent to our word "hell?" By no means; for "hell" is the name we give to the final estate of the wicked; to us it suggests, whatever it may have suggested to an earlier generation, the thought of never-ending punishment. But our Lord, in his parable, is evidently speaking only of the state which immediately follows death. Neither Lazarus nor Nimeusis (if this were the rich man's name) has reached his last state, his final condition, or can reach it until after the day on which the secrets of all hearts shall be disclosed. So that even here we must reject the word "hell," and retain Christ's word, "hades."

Nor is our Lord's description of the moral effects of the "torment" on the Rich Man's character without many suggestions of hope, were this the place to dwell on them. For obviously a process of amendment has begun to take effect on him, and even now already has been carried to a surprising length. He who had cared only for himself now cares for his "five brethren," and cares not that they should be clothed with purple and fine linen, and surfeited with sumptuous fare, but that they should be quickened and renewed in the spirit of their minds, and saved from the torment to which he has doomed himself. In short, vital and hopeful germs of charity and spirituality have already been released and developed within him; and how can any torment, any discipline, which produces such happy effects, be enduring?

Turn now to Acts ii. 27 and 31. In his great sermon on the Day of Pentecost, St Peter is arguing that Jesus of Nazareth was the Christ whose advent had been afore-announced by the Hebrew prophets. He quotes certain words uttered by "the patriarch David," which he affirms were true of Jesus, and of Him alone—"Thou wilt not leave thy Holy One *in Hades.*" In those words, argues the Apostle, David "spake of the resurrection of Christ, that *his* soul was not left *in Hades.*" Now here, surely, every man may see for himself how inaccurate and misleading it is to translate "Hades" by "Hell." God will not *leave* his Holy One, the Christ, *in hell!* Is *that* a promise? What special grace is there, or rather, is there not a very special and incredible indignity, in assuring the Holy One that God will not *leave Him* in hell, when we know that He will not suffer any of his holy ones so much as to enter hell? But though God does not suffer any good man to enter hell, He suffers all good men to enter Hades. He *leaves* them there, in the world of disembodied spirits, until the morning of the resurrection; *i.e.*, He leaves them all there *but one*. The Christ could not be holden of death; his soul was not left in Hades, as ours are, any more than his flesh saw corruption, as ours does. There was, therefore, a very special grace in the promise made to Him, a grace vouchsafed to none but Him; and if this promise were fulfilled in Jesus of Nazareth, as St Peter affirmed it was, its fulfilment was an infallible proof that he was in very deed the Christ of God.[1]

[1] There is one other passage in the *Textus Receptus* in which Hades occurs; but here (1 Cor. xv. 55) the Authorized Version renders it by "grave." The true Text, however, reads $\theta \acute{a} \nu a \tau \eta$ (*death*), not ᾅδε (*Hades*).

There are also four places in the Apocalypse in which "hell" is substituted for "Hades," in our Version. They are as follows:—Rev. i. 18, "I have the keys of *Hades* and of Death;" Rev. vi. 8, "His name that sat on him was Death, and *Hades* followed with him;" Rev. xx. 13, "Death and *Hades* delivered up the dead that were in them;" and Rev. xx. 14, "Death and *Hades* were cast into the lake of fire." No real student of the Bible will deny that the word Hades should be retained in all these cases. And indeed one is puzzled to know what those who hold the "orthodox" view can possibly make of the last of these texts, if they retain the present rendering of it; for surely "the lake of fire" stands for hell; and if hades also be hell, it would seem that *hell* was, or is to be, *cast into hell*,—a somewhat questionable feat.

Now these are all the passages in the Gospels and the Epistles in which the word Hades occurs; and I think you will admit that in no one of these cases should it be translated by the word "hell." For whereas our word "hell" denotes the final and everlasting torment of the wicked, there is not a single instance in which the word "Hades" is used in that sense. Where it applies to the lot of the wicked at all, it denotes simply that intermediate and preparatory state of punishment, or discipline, which precedes "the last judgment;" while at least, in some cases, the word obviously covers *Paradise* as well as *Gehenna*, and denotes the tranquil and happy intermediate estate of the good, that rest-full region or condition in which the righteous await the Resurrection, and into which Christ Himself entered, although He was not "left" in it.

3. There is but one other word in the New Testament which is rendered by "hell," the word *Gehenna*. This word occurs twelve times in the Gospels and Epistles. And how inadequately the word "hell" translates it you will see if we consider (1) the derivation of the word; (2) the sense in which it was used and understood in the time of our Lord and his Apostles; and (3) the meaning of the several passages in which it is found. And as these passages are those on which the popular dogma is very largely based, we must examine them with some patience and care.

(1). As to the derivation of the word there is not, there never has been, the slightest doubt. *Gehenna* is the Greek form of the Hebrew *Ge-Hinnom,* or "Valley of Hinnom." This valley was a steep ravine immediately under the South-Western wall of Jerusalem, watered by the brook Kidron and "Siloa's sacred stream." In the time of the Hebrew Kings it was laid out in "paradises," *i.e.,* pleasure gardens, with their groves, pools, fish-ponds. Here the wealthier nobles and citizens of Jerusalem had their country villas, their summer palaces. At its South-Eastern extremity lay the paradise of King Solomon, with its "tophet," or music grove, the grove in which the King, with his wives and concubines, listened to his men-singers and women-singers, and to the blended strains of "musical instruments of divers sorts." The whole beautiful valley, in short, was full of those delicious retreats which are still found in the close neighbourhood of large and wealthy Oriental cities, and in which the monarch and his nobles seek repose from the sultry heat of the summer, and from the frets and toils of public life. To gratify the "foreign women" with whom he consorted, Solomon polluted his pleasant gardens and groves with idolatrous shrines, in which the cruel and licentious rites of Egypt and Phœnicia were observed. His successors imitated, and out-ran, his evil example. The horrid fires of Molech were kindled in the beautiful valley, and children were burned in them—" passed through the fire." Gradually " the valley of Hinnom " grew to be a type of all that was flagrantly wicked and abominable to the faithful souls, fallen on evil times, who still worshipped Jehovah on the neighbouring hill of Zion. And when Josiah came to the throne, and good men could once more lift up their heads, the groves were burned down, the pleasant gardens laid waste, the shrines ground to powder, and, to render the valley for ever " unclean," the bones of the dead were strewn over its surface. Thenceforth it became the common cesspool of the city, into which offal was cast, and the carcasses of animals, and even the bodies of great criminals who had lived a life so vile as to be judged unworthy of decent burial. Worms preyed on their corrupting flesh ; and fires were kept burning lest the pestilential infection should rise from the valley and float through the streets of Jerusalem.

To the Hebrew prophets this foul terrible Valley became an apt type, or illustration, of the doom of the unrighteous. They drew from it their images, images of which such terrible and unwarrantable use has been made, of the worm that never dies, and of the fire which is not quenched. With them, to say that a man was in danger of Gehenna was to say that his sins had exposed him to a judgment the terrors of which were faintly shadowed forth by the sickening horrors of the detestable Ge-Hinnom.

(2). This is the derivation of the word. In what sense it was used and understood in the time of Christ and his Apostles, it is not so easy to say. To determine that point requires no little learning and research. But we may reasonably conclude that, if we *can* recover the sense in which the word was commonly used by the Jews some nineteen centuries ago, we may be sure that *that* is the sense in which Christ used it; for we cannot doubt that He would have defined the word afresh, that He would openly have put a new sense into it, unless He used it in the sense in which his hearers already understood it. Whatever certain modern teachers and ministers may do, we may be quite sure that the Great Teacher did not use in one sense words which He knew that those who listened to Him took in another and a very different sense.

Now, all the Jewish writings which date from three centuries before Christ to three centuries after Christ have been carefully ransacked, with a view to ascertain the meaning then placed on the word Gehenna.[1] And

---

[1] Among others, and chief among those who have ransacked the Hebrew literature of this period, with an express view of determining the significance of Gehenna, I may mention the Rev. Alfred Dewes, D.D., LL.D., perpetual curate of St Augustine's, Pendlebury, Manchester, who has published the result of his researches in a

the result of the search—a result confirmed to me personally by that eminent Hebrew scholar, Emmanuel small volume, not so well known as it deserves to be, entitled "A Plea for a New Translation of the Scriptures." To him I am indebted for the references which follow, and for many hints which have helped me to make this and the next sub-division of my Lecture more complete. In order that my readers may know more exactly the ground covered, and the care with which it has been covered, by this erudite and laborious scholar, I cite a few sentences from his work. After animadverting on the "rather pitiable way" in which one Commentator after another has defined and repeated Lightfoot's somewhat ambiguous words, taking him to assert, or making him assert, "that Gehenna was the abode of the damned, a place of eternal fire, and that there are endless examples to prove it," he adds (p. 21): "With a view to test the truth of an assertion so continually made, the present writer has searched all the Jewish writings that can with any probability be assigned to any date within three centuries from our Saviour's birth. *And whenever he asserts that an idea is not to be found in any work, he wishes it to be understood that the whole work has been read through, not that its index only has been searched.* It did not seem worth while to read any of the later Jewish works; it was quite out of the question to think of wading through the Talmuds; but the earlier of them is assigned to the middle of the fourth century and the later to the end of the fifth. Every passage, however, has been carefully examined even from them, which is quoted in the works of Lightfoot, Schoettgen, Buxtorf, Castell, Schindler, Glass, Bartoloccius, Ugalino, and Nork: *and the result of the whole examination is this: there are but two passages which even a superficial reader could consider to be corroborative of the assertion that the Jews understood Gehenna to be a place of everlasting punishment.*" Among the works read by Dr Dewes were, of course, the several books of the Apocrypha, the writings of Philo and Josephus, the Targums, and, as he has said, those passages in the Talmuds which are commonly cited in favour of the popular dogma. And surely it is a wonderful result of his examination of these and other works that only two sentences—I only know of one (*i.e.*, in the Talmud)—were discovered which even appeared to favour that dogma, and that neither of these, when investigated, could be held to lend it any support.

Deutsch[1]—is that, without a single exception, or with only one very doubtful exception,[2] these writings lend no countenance to, that they positively discountenance, the English translation of that word. That is to say, the uninspired Jewish writings for the six centuries nearest to Christ know nothing, absolutely nothing, of "hell." What, then, do we find in these writings? We constantly find such sentences as

[1] On the only occasion on which I had the privilege and pleasure of a long talk with Mr Deutsch, I cited as many of the passages adduced by Dr Dewes as I could recall, and asked him whether the impression in his mind at all harmonized with the conclusion to which these citations naturally led. His answer, given very emphatically, was that they very fairly represented the teaching of the Jewish rabbis; and he added, "Of this you may be quite sure, that there is not a word in the Talmud which lends any support to that damnable dogma of endless torment." Since then his incomparable essay on the Talmud has been given to the world, and in that essay this private opinion of his is publicly affirmed. So that if any one should think that Dr Dewes might have found passages in the Talmud, had he searched it for himself, which would have modified his conclusion, Mr Deutsch comes to the rescue, and declares, with all the authority of his unrivalled knowledge of the Talmud, that it throws its whole weight in favour of that conclusion, and not against it.

[2] This one exception is a sentence from the Talmud (Rosc. hasciana, ch. I.), which declares that "*Christians and apostates descend into Gehenna, and are judged in it for generations of generations.*" But the passage is of late date; it is obviously inspired by the hatred and scorn felt by the Jewish rabbis for those Christians who seek to "convert" Jews, and for those Jews who apostatize from the faith of their fathers: and, after all, "generations of generations" is not precisely equivalent to "for ever and for ever." It is a fine sign of Mr Deutsch's fairness that even in his brief abstract of the Talmudic teaching on this point, he includes in it the solitary passage which seems opposed to its general spirit (see his "Remains," p. 53).

these: " Gehenna is ordained of old because of sins."[1]
" In Gehenna the fire is kindled every day."[2] " God hath prepared Gehenna for the ungodly who transgress his commandments."[3] " The ungodly will be judged in Gehenna, to shew that there is none in whom is the virtue of innocence *against the day of judgment.*"[3] " The ungodly shall be judged in Gehenna *until the righteous shall say of them, We have seen enough!*"[4] " The judgment of the ungodly is *for twelve months.*"[5] " Noah, seeing the Angel of Death, hid himself in the ark twelve months, *because the judgment on sinners lasts for twelve months.*"[6] " The impious shall be burned up by the heat of the sun."[7] " *Gehenna is nothing but a day* in which the impious will be burned."[8] " The sinners of Israel and the sinners of the Gentiles shall descend with the body into Gehenna, *and for twelve months shall be condemned in it;* at the end of twelve months the body shall be consumed, and the soul burned up, and the wind shall scatter it under the feet of the just."[9]

Now, of course, these ancient Hebrew sayings carry no authority on points of Christian doctrine. We are not to take them as yielding any real help to *our*

[1] Targum of Jonathan Ben Uzziel on Isaiah xxx. 33.
[2] *Ibid.*, on lxv. 5.   [3] *Ibid.*, on 1 Samuel ii. 8, 9.
[4] *Ibid.*, on Isaiah lxvi. 24.   [5] Mishna, Adyoth, ch. 2, *s.* 9.
[6] The Cabalistic Book of Zohar, col. 205.
[7] Talmud, Avodah Zarah, ch. 1.
[8] [9] Talmud, Rosc. hasciana, ch. 1.

theory of the future life. Nay, as Bartoloccius, in his "Bibliotheca Rabbinica," long since complained, "the propositions which they contain are so variable and unstable" that "no firm and unshifting dogma can be deduced from them" as to the future punishment of the guilty. But this much we may learn from them, as he reluctantly confesses, that the Jewish rabbis did not believe in "a material fire," and that they thought such fire as they did believe in would one day be put out.[1] And the conclusion of this learned Talmudist is abundantly confirmed by the most eminent and erudite Hebraist of our own day, Emmanuel Deutsch. In his celebrated essay on the Talmud, he writes[2] : "*There is no everlasting damnation according to the Talmud. There is only a temporary punishment even for the worst of sinners.* 'Generations upon generations' shall last the damnation of idolaters, apostates, and traitors. But there is a space of 'only two fingers' breadth between hell and heaven;' the sinner has but to repent sincerely, and the gates to everlasting bliss will spring open. No human being is excluded from the world to come. Every man, of whatever creed or nation, provided he be of the righteous, shall be admitted into it."

And there is another point on which these sentences

---

[1] See Dr Dewes' *Plea*, pp. 23, 24.
[2] Literary Remains, p. 53.

of the Jewish Fathers speak with high and conclusive authority; they shew us, they prove beyond contradiction the general sense put on the word Gehenna by the Jews of our Lord's time. Obviously they thought of Gehenna as the state in which the wicked would be reserved for judgment, as an intermediate, not the final, state. On the duration of that state of punishment, or discipline, they differed, as also on its ultimate issue. Some held that the torment of Gehenna would endure for twelve months; some, for a single day; some, only until the righteous should desire it to end —and *that* surely would not be very long. And, again, some held that the discipline of Gehenna would issue in the ultimate salvation of all who were exposed to it; while others held that it would issue in their destruction, the very souls of sinners being burned up and scattered by the wind. With these differences of opinion we are not at present concerned. All we have to mark is the general sense in which the word Gehenna was then used and understood; and I do not see how we are to escape the conclusion that among the Jews it was taken to denote a punishment, or discipline, which did not extend beyond a definite, and probably a very short, period of time. Christ was a Jew, and spoke to Jews; and in what but their Jewish sense can we fairly and reasonably interpret his words?

(3). Taking the word in this Jewish sense, as we are bound to do, let us briefly examine the Scriptures in which it occurs. The word Gehenna is used eleven times by our Lord, and once by his "brother" James. No other of the Apostles, or Apostolic men, uses it even once, mainly, no doubt, because they wrote to *Gentile* churches, to whom this Jewish word, this illustration taken from the immediate vicinity of Jerusalem, would have been strange and perplexing.

The first instance in which it is employed is St Matthew v. 22. Christ is comparing his laws, the laws of the kingdom of heaven, with the laws given of old time by Moses. Moses had said, "Thou shalt not kill, and whosoever shall kill shall be in danger of the judgment. But," continues Christ, "*I* say unto you, Whosoever is angry with his brother without a cause shall be in danger of the judgment; and whosoever shall say to his brother Raca (a mere expletive of disgust and contempt, like the odious expletives which we may hear every day in our own streets) shall be in danger of the Council: but whosoever shall say, Thou fool, shall be in danger of *hell-fire.*" The general sense of the passage is that, whereas Moses condemned murder, Christ condemns the angry passions in which murder takes its rise. Even an angry emotion was henceforth to be regarded as incipient murder; and if that angry emotion found vent in angry and malicious words, words which smote and wounded a neighbour's heart, it was to be held a still heavier crime, worthy of a still severer punishment. This, confessedly, is the general sense of our Lord's saying; but he casts his thought in a technical and figurative form which needs a little explanation.

In every Jewish city there were courts of justice[1] which had the power of life and death; but, though they could condemn criminals to death *by the sword*, they had no authority to inflict that death *by stoning* which was the most ignominious punishment known to the Hebrew code. Only the Sanhedrin, the supreme council at Jerusalem, could inflict that penalty. But the Sanhedrin, besides condemning a man to be stoned, could also ordain that, after death, his body should be cast into the valley of Hinnom, to become the prey of the worm or of the fire. We hold it a bitter disgrace to be denied Christian burial; but for a Jew to be denied burial in the family sepulchre, and thus not to be "gathered to his fathers," was far more shameful and terrible. Of these national customs and feelings our Lord avails Himself in the passage before us. He affirms that whoso is angry with his brother without a cause shall be in danger of, shall put himself in the power of, those local courts of justice which sat in every city, wielding the power of life and death.

[1] Deut. xvi. 18; and Josephus, *Ant.* iv. 8, 14; *Wars*, ii. 20, 3.

He affirms that whoso vents his spleen in the expletive "Raca" shall be in danger of the Sanhedrin, the metropolitan court, or " council," which alone could condemn men to be stoned. And He also affirms that whoso vents his anger in the word "Fool" shall be liable to be condemned after death to "*the Gehenna of fire*," *i.e.*, to the valley of Hinnom, in which the fires were always at work on the refuse of the city.[1]

This is the form in which the Lord Jesus cast that law of his kingdom which forbids causeless anger, and the contemptuous or malicious words in which it finds expression. But consider, first, how the word "hell" introduces a false tone and scale into the law of Christ. Here are three sins and three punishments. The three sins are anger, the anger that says Raca, and the anger that says Fool—a somewhat harsher and more contemptuous word, at least in Hebrew ears. And the three punishments are that of the local court, that of the metropolitan court, and that of hell-fire! Now between the three sins there is a gradual descent,

---

[1] All this is as well brought out probably as it can be by a mere translation in Mr M'Clellan's new Translation of the Gospels, which runs thus:—
21. "Ye have heard that it was said unto them of old time,
  'Thou shalt do no murder:
And whosoever shall do murder shall be liable to the judges.'
22. But I say unto you, Every one that is angry with his brother shall be liable to the judges: and whosoever shall say to his brother, 'Tush!' shall be liable to the High Council: and whosoever shall say, 'Thou fool,' shall be liable for the Burning Valley of Fire."

each is a little worse than the one which goes before it. But who does not feel that in the three punishments, instead of a correspondingly gradual descent, there is, in the last interval, a sudden plunge so vast, so profound, as to be out of all keeping. The disproportion strikes one in two ways. It is incredible that to call a man Fool should be so much worse a crime than to call him Raca that, whereas for the one offence men are to be brought before a court of justice, for the other they are to be damned to an everlasting torment. And it is equally incredible that any man should be doomed to all the horrors of hell if, in a moment of angry impulse, he let the word Fool, or any other word, slip from his lips. On the other hand, if for "hell-fire" we read "Gehenna of fire," and understand that, while the first punishment is that which a local court may inflict—death, and the second that which only the metropolitan court can inflict—death by stoning, the third is to be cast out, unburied, into the accursed valley of Hinnom, we at least restore something like scale and proportion to the sentence, though the punishments still look, if not far too heavy, far too material and external for the sins.

And, indeed, if any man really studies these words, he soon finds it quite impossible to take them in their literal sense. In *that* sense they are not true. No Jew, no Christian was ever brought before a local court of justice, and condemned to be beheaded simply for indulging an angry thought or feeling. No Jew, no Christian was ever called before the Sanhedrin, and condemned to be stoned to death simply for calling his brother Raca. No Jew, no Christian was ever first put to a shameful death, and then denied decent burial, simply for calling his brother Fool. And no man who reads these words with the understanding can for a moment suppose that Christ meant these sins of anger to be brought before courts of justice, and to be visited with punishments so disproportioned and inappropriate. The most savage judge who ever disgraced the bench would not have doomed men to death for an angry feeling that was never uttered in word or action, nor to a death in the last degree shameful for uttering an angry word. And would *Christ*, the Lover and Redeemer of men? Use your common sense. Translate these Hebrew figures of speech into their English equivalents, and see what you think of them then. "Whosoever is angry with his brother without cause shall be brought up before the Police Court; and whosoever shall call his neighbour Coxcomb shall be tried for his life at the Assizes: and whosoever shall call his brother Fool shall be hung, and then denied Christian burial!" Can you swallow that? Does *that* sound like "the sweet reasonableness of Christ" to you? If not, you may be sure that He who taught all things in parables is uttering a parable here. There is no thought of hell in his mind; there is no thought even of literal courts of justice. He is simply teaching an Oriental people, in the Oriental forms with which they were familiar, that every sin, however inward, will receive its due recompense of reward; that the heart is the fountain from which all sin flows; that in God's sight the murderous wish, scheme, bent, *is* murder: and that every utterance of it, whether in word or in deed, since it deepens and confirms it, will entail a still severer punishment. "Be angry, and you will suffer for it; let your anger mount to utterance, and you will suffer the more: every new access and expression of evil passion will plunge you still deeper in sin and misery." *This* is what Christ meant; *this* is the law of anger as interpreted by Him.

Twice more the word Gehenna is used by Christ in the Sermon on the Mount (St Matthew v. 29 and 30). If our right eye or our right hand offend us, if, that is, it become an occasion of sin, we are to cut it off or to pluck it out; for "it is profitable for thee that one of thy members should perish, and not that thy whole body should be cast into *Gehenna*." It is the law of Adultery of which our Lord speaks here; and He treats it in precisely the same method and spirit in which we have already heard Him treat the law of Murder. The Jewish code only punished the outward overt act—punished it by stoning, and in aggravated cases by dooming the bodies of the offenders to be flung into the valley of Hinnom. Our Lord used this Jewish punishment to illustrate his meaning. "To commit adultery is," He says, "to take the way to Gehenna. And as I adjudge even a lustful look, or touch, to be adultery, it were better for you to pluck out your right eye, or to cut off your most serviceable hand, than to commit that sin; since, by the loss of one member, you may save your whole body from the fire and the worm."

*Can* we take these words in their literal sense? or are not they too a parable? If we take the word Gehenna literally, as meaning the valley of Hinnom, we must also take the right eye and the right hand literally; and every man who has looked and longed and touched must cut off his hand and pluck out his eye. Is *that* what Christ means? Is *his* code written in blood? Does *He* bid us atone the sin of the soul by mutilating the body? Impossible! The simple truth is that no thought of a literal valley of horrors was in his mind, and still less any thought of an everlasting torment, to be evaded only by an excision of the offending organs of sense. He was simply using these familiar terms as figures of speech to convey the solemn warning, that it is better for us to endure the utmost pains of self-denial and self-restraint than to yield even to the first movements of sensual and unlawful desire.

A similar passage occurs in St Matthew xviii. 8 and 9, and is repeated, in an expanded form, in St Mark ix. 43-48. In both we are exhorted to cut off the hand, the foot, the eye which offends, on the ground that it is better for us to go into life maimed and halt and blind than to have our whole body cast into *Gehenna*—" *into the Gehenna where their worm dieth not and the fire is not quenched.*" Here, of course, the allusion is not to hell, but to the valley of Hinnom outside Jerusalem, where fires were always burning and the worm for ever preyed on the corpses of the dead. And here, again, there is *only* an allusion to that valley; *i.e.*, Gehenna is only a figure of speech. For if we take any part of the passage literally, we must take it literally throughout. If Gehenna stands for a real valley, polluted by the prey of the worm and the fire, then in common fairness we must admit that the foot and the hand and the eye stand for the physical organs and members of the human frame, and the plucking out and cutting off for real physical acts. But we cannot take the whole passage in that literal way. It is impossible that we should please God by maiming and crippling the body which He has given us. And how should *our* whole body, the bodies of English men and women, be cast into a Palestinian valley?

What our Lord is really teaching here is one of the first and most important moral lessons we all have to master, viz., that we must learn to go without a great many things we should like to have; that we must learn to rule and deny ourselves on pain of being ruined and undone. What He means is that self-control, self-denial, is life to us; that self-seeking, unbridled self-indulgence, is death. If we deny ourselves our strongest craving when to indulge it would be wrong, if we refuse to yield to our most absorbing affection when to gratify it we must sin against God and our neighbour and wrong our own souls, we enter into our true life, into the life which is eternal; and enter into it *here and now*. We may indeed enter into this life maimed and wounded for a time; for have we not crucified our strongest craving, our most engrossing affection, that we might enter it? Nevertheless, even on these terms, it is well to lay hold upon life, or to seize it in a firmer grasp. But if we care mainly to please ourselves, to gratify instead of ruling our passions and desires; if we *will* take our own way and follow our own will at the cost of conscience and duty, we lose our true life; we adjudge ourselves unworthy of it: *here and now* we enter into the eternal death, for here and now we cut ourselves off from God and his eternal life of service and self-sacrifice. *This*, without a figure, is the general principle which our Lord taught in figures intelligible and acceptable to the Jewish mind.

As yet, then, we have not met a single passage which so much as alludes to the future state of the wicked. But you will find such a passage in St Matthew x. 28, which is repeated in St Luke xii. 5. St Matthew represents Christ as saying, "Fear not them which kill the body, but are not able to kill the soul; but rather fear him who is able to destroy both soul and body *in Gehenna.*" St Luke reports Him as saying, "Be not afraid of those that kill the body, and after that have no more that they can do; but I will forewarn you whom ye shall fear: fear him who, after he hath killed, hath power to cast *into the Gehenna.*" Now as the disciples listened to this impressive warning, in what sense would they understand it? what thoughts and associations would it quicken in their minds? They had been trained to believe that at death the souls of the unrighteous would descend into a frightful region in much resembling the polluted and abhorred Valley outside the walls of Jerusalem; that they would suffer dreadful torments in it for a brief space of time: and that then their very souls would be burned up and scattered, like dust by a wind, under the feet of the just. They would therefore understand Christ to mean that, because men could only kill the body, they were not so much to be feared as God, who could destroy both body and soul in Gehenna: they would understand that it was better for them to dare the utmost wrath of man than to sin against God. But can it be right to translate the word "Gehenna," in which after brief torment both soul and body might be destroyed, by our word "hell," when, for us at least, "hell" is the name of a place in which both body and soul are not destroyed, but kept alive for ever in order that they may for ever be tormented in its flame?

In St Matthew xxiii. 15, our Lord pronounces a woe on the Scribes and Pharisees because they compassed sea and land to make one proselyte, and, when they had got him, "ye make him twofold more *a son of Gehenna* than yourselves." In Verse 33 of the same Chapter He demands of them, "How shall ye escape *the judgment of Gehenna?*" Both these phrases are of frequent recurrence in Jewish literature. "A son of Gehenna" meant very much what "Son of Shaitan" means in the East now, viz., a wicked and abandoned man, "a child of the devil," a man born again from below rather than from above. "The judgment of Gehenna" was the sentence to the torment and destruction of Gehenna—the verdict by which a man was doomed to be stoned in the valley of Hinnom, his body being left to the worm, the jackal, the raven, and the flame; or, when used in a figurative sense, the sentence to the darker region of the Hadean world. Neither phrase has any meaning at all resembling that of our word "hell." What our Lord intended was that the Pharisees *corrupted* the proselytes they were so zealous to make—"out of bad heathen making worse Jews," as Erasmus puts it; corrupted them by teaching them to veil greed, perjury, uncleanness, and even murder itself, behind a mask of religion: and that they themselves, therefore, deserved that very sentence to the death and horrors of Ge-Hinnom to which they were so ready to doom men far less guilty than themselves.

The last passage in which the word occurs is James iii. 6. "The tongue is a fire; .... it defileth the whole body, both setting on fire the whole round of nature and being set on fire *of Gehenna.*" And here, obviously, the meaning is that the unruly and malicious tongue, which kindles a fire wherever it falls, is like those noxious and infectious flames which burned night and day in the loathsome valley of Hinnom, or that it is tipped with that searching and destructive flame which, as the Jews thought, destroys both the body and the soul of the prisoners in the unseen world.

We have now examined every passage in the New Testament in which the word Gehenna occurs. We have found that for the most part it is used in a purely figurative sense; that, so often as it is used in a literal sense, it denotes the punishments executed on criminal Jews in this present world: and that, in the one or two cases, in which it veils a reference to the punishments of the world to come, it would be understood by those who heard it as denoting that brief agony which, as they thought, would precede the entire destruction of the wicked. And, therefore, the word "hell," in the sense in which we use it, is in every case a monstrous mistranslation of the word "Gehenna," and should be replaced by it. It is quite possible that, if the word Gehenna were transferred to our Version, many would be perplexed by it at first, as at first many were arrested by the Greek word "baptism." It is very probable that, for a time at least, its exact shade of meaning would be disputed, just as there are still those who dispute the meaning of "baptism." But these would be slight evils as compared with the immense evil of retaining the word "hell," the meaning of which every reader fancies he knows, but the meaning of which, at least in the sense in which it is now commonly taken, is utterly alien to the mind of our Lord and his Apostles.

Nay, as we have also seen, neither the Lord Jesus nor his Apostles had any such word as "hell" in their vocabulary, or any conception answering to it in their thoughts. The only words they use are *Tartarus*, which stands for the classical conception of an underworld, in which the shades of the dead enjoy some poor shadow of their former joys or suffer some faint shadow of their former woes; *Hades*, which stands for the Jewish conception of a similar underworld in which the souls of the good and of the bad alike await the trumpet of the Resurrection; and *Gehenna*, which stands for that dark province of the underworld in which the souls of the unrighteous are tormented for a time, and until it shall please God to put an end to their misery.

The word "hell," therefore, has no sort of right to a place in our Bible; and I cannot and will not doubt that those of you who have long felt that the dogma of an everlasting punishment inflicted for the sins of time threw dark shadows on the very throne, nay, on the very character, of God, will thankfully expunge it from the Inspired Record. But do not too hastily assume that, by getting rid of the word "hell," you also get rid of the doctrine of retribution. To sin *is* to suffer even here and now, and will be to suffer hereafter. No man can be freed from sin except by suffering, as our daily experience and observation of life plentifully avouch. And if any man abide in sin to the very last moment, we may well believe that he will then enter into a suffering so intense and so protracted as that he may feel it had been better for him had he never been born. The merciful God, simply because He is merciful, does not shrink from inflicting any pain upon us which is necessary to our welfare, even in this world; and if the sufferings of this world fail to cleanse us from evil, what possible alternative do we leave Him but to inflict sufferings still more penetrative and cleansing in the world to come? No man who at all knows the evil of his own heart, and how hard it is to get quit of it; no man even who has slipped into a passing indulgence of sinful and exorbitant passion, which was pleasant enough for the moment and did not then seem so very wrong, can recall the shame, the agony, the remorse in which even a momentary sin has landed him, and doubt that habitual and unrepented sins will entail a misery well-nigh, if not altogether, intolerable. But to endure sufferings imposed by Love for our deliverance from evil is one thing; and to endure sufferings which do not tend to correct and amend us, which only harden and degrade us, and which are to know no close, is another and a very different thing. A wise man might well take it as the dearest proof of Divine Love that God should expose him to the severest agonies requisite for his own well-being, and much more for the welfare of the world at large; but how can any thoughtful man reconcile the infliction of intolerable and never-ceasing anguish either on those who sinned and knew not what they did, or even on those who knew what they did when they sinned, with the love or with the very justice of God? That the wrath of God should be revealed from heaven against all unrighteousness of men in this and all other worlds, I can well believe, and can even see that such a wrath as that is but a severer form of love; but that the just God dooms men to abide in sin for ever because they have sinned for a few hours of time, with no prospect of amendment and no hope of relief,—how am I to believe *that*, if at least I am to believe in God at all, and to love Him as the sole and ever-springing fountain of that Charity which covers a multitude of sins?

Still there are many who, despite this perplexity of thought, this impossibility of reconciling the justice no less than the love of God with the everlasting damnation of the vast majority of men, fear to renounce that horrible dogma lest, by renouncing it, they should perilously reduce and abridge the terrors of retribution, and thus leave men at ease in their sins. They hold, and hold rightly, that sin ought to be, and must be, punished: but they do not see that the punishment which is the present, the natural, and inevitable consequence of sin is the true death, the true hell; and that to be unconscious of this punishment is itself the worst punishment of all. They see a man who has lived for the flesh and the things of the flesh, but who has only indulged his passions within the limits of a certain moderation and decorum—never caused any grave scandal nor entangled himself in the web of law, never exposed himself to the ban of social reprobation and exclusion. He prospers and enjoys himself; he is "fat and flourishing." So that he makes a fortune, rises in the social scale, is held in fair repute and can command the luxuries and recreations to which he has accustomed himself, he is quite content with himself and his lot. He looks for nothing higher, cares for nothing better. And as they consider him they are grieved and perplexed; they ask, "Where is the judgment of God?" Where is it! Why, *there, in the man himself, and in his base content with a lot so base.* He is content though he lives only to pamper his senses and indulge the pride of life; content though he, an heir of immortality, lives only for earth and time, and though all that is noblest and best in his nature is dwindling for lack of use! He thinks more of his business or profession, more even of his cricketing and fishing and shooting, nay, more of his very dinner, than of mental culture, or moral sweetness and purity, or of the sacred and august realities of eternity. Deeming himself among the manliest of men, he is of all men the most unmanly—*i.e.*, the least like the true Man, the perfect Man. His base content with himself is but the numbness and torpor of a disease which draws nigh to death. Under heaven and before men there is no creature more degraded, and fallen from high estate, than he—a capable and immortal spirit pining toward death under the tyranny of lusts and cravings he was born to rule. And yet, fools and blind that we are, we ask, "Where is the judgment of God? why are the sinful prosperous and at ease?" Their very prosperity, such as it is, and their content with it, are, as the Psalmist long since perceived, their ruin and destruction.

Is it not punishment enough for men that they should have so miserably fallen from their "pride of place"? If not, think of them when they go hence—deprived of the senses through which they have drawn in all their delights, hurried into the world of spirits with spirits stained, polluted, debased, unbroken to spiritual toils, insensitive to spiritual joys, unsustained by spiritual hopes;—think of them, I say, when they pass into a world all strange, alien, repulsive to them: will they not suffer then? Can *they* find a home and its sanctities in Hades? can they find a Paradise and its joys? Will it not be a most miserable Gehenna to them? Must they not then fear Him who *has* destroyed their bodies, and is still able to destroy their souls? Ah, we need not "fret because of evil doers and be envious against the workers of iniquity;" we need not fear lest that natural sense of justice which calls for the due punishment of wickedness should be ungratified. If we are men and possess the capable and forecasting spirit proper to man, can we not penetrate these hindering veils of flesh and custom, and see in the moral loss and spiritual degradation of those who are without God in the world a punishment all the more terrible because they are unconscious of it, and make no effort to escape it? Can we not project ourselves so far into the future as to anticipate the time when, flesh and heart having failed them, they will have become only too sadly conscious of their degradation and woe? Can we not resolve that as for us, God helping us, *we* will not sink into the present hell of spiritual death, and lay up for ourselves a fearful looking-for of judgment?

For, consider, this intelligent contriving soul of ours, which we acknowledge to be " the master part of us," —did God intend it to find its true satisfaction and rest in pleasures which perish as we enjoy them, or in a world for ever on the flux and that will soon pass away? *Can* we find our chief good, our true rest and peace, save in that which is as enduring as ourselves? When we die all that is material and temporal in us is resolved into the elements from which it sprang; " our bodies to earth, our blood to water, heat to fire, breath to air:" but *mind*—but *thought*—but *the soul* which informed all—what will become of *these?* " Where will *they* find their parent element, who will call *them* home?" "*We* shall still be in them, and they in us;"[1] but these are not material, not sensual: they can find no home in the material universe. And if we have made them the mere captives and hungry dependants of sense, how can they but go out into a world all strange, and alien, and full of torment? Is it wise, then, to neglect this our master part? *Is* he a true man who sacrifices that which is highest and most enduring in him to that which is most fugitive and lowest? Is not *he* dead even while he lives, and damned even before he is judged?

[1] The citations are from Matthew Arnold's *Empedocles on Etna,* Act ii. pp. 64, 65.

# V.—THE CHRISTIAN DOCTRINE OF THE ÆONS.

We have now examined all the passages in the Gospels and Epistles in which the words "hell" and "damnation" occur. We have found that these words are always a false and misleading translation of the original words of Scripture, since the two verbs rendered by "to damn" never mean more than "to judge" and "to condemn;" while the three substantives rendered by "hell"—"Tartarus," "Hades," and "Gehenna"—all indicate a temporary and intermediate state, not a final and everlasting state.

The second class of Scriptures we have to examine is that in which the words "eternal" and "everlasting" occur; and in this class a subordinate series in which, as these epithets are applied both to the future felicity of the good and the future misery of the wicked, the logical inference seems to be that the one will last as long as the other.

Now this class of passages is so numerous, the words "eternal," "everlasting," "for ever," and the like recur so frequently, that it will be simply impossible for us to examine them all. We must be content with some general remarks which will cover them all, and with a detailed investigation of a few leading texts which bear most directly on the subject we have in hand.

And perhaps the very first point we should mark is this: that, though the words "eternal" and "everlasting" are used indiscriminately to translate one and the same Greek word, they are by no means identical in meaning. The word "eternal" bears two great meanings, and is used in two very different senses. Popularly and loosely it is used to denote that which lasts for ever; but as it is used by many of our most eminent thinkers and theologians, instead of denoting that which endures through all the successions of time, it denotes that which is *above and beyond* time, that which is independent of duration; that which you can no more calculate on the sequences of time than you can weigh music by the pound or measure beauty with a foot-rule. God, for example, and Christ, and indeed all that pertains to the spiritual realm—as faith, hope, charity, righteousness, peace—are eternal in this higher sense.[1] They cannot be expressed in terms of

[1] It must be admitted however that this higher sense has been put into the word: it is not the original meaning of the word: according to its derivation "eternal" means "age-long" (see page 119). And if it could be brought back to its original meaning, if it now suggested nothing more, it would be the very word of all words for rendering the Greek αἰώνιος. But *that*, I suppose, is wholly impossible.

duration. They cannot be brought within the measures of time. God may indeed, and does, act within the limits of time; but He is not confined by them. Faith and love may be quickened and experienced in the hours of time; but they are not to be measured and limited by its sequences and changes. They are spiritual, eternal.

Now this meaning of the word "eternal," as denoting that which transcends the standards and limits of time, that which is above and beyond, before and after it, that which encompasses as well as penetrates and suffuses it, is clearly the greater and the nobler of the two; it is even held by some modern teachers and theologians to be the only meaning in which the word should now be employed. So that we must not take the words "eternal" and "everlasting" as synonyms or equivalents. The one indicates that which continues through the whole of duration; the other, that which is out of duration and above it, of which the measures and sequences of time are no necessary part. The one expresses *quantity*, the other *quality*. "Everlasting" denotes that which lasts for ever; "eternal," that which is spiritual and divine. And hence to translate one and the same Greek word by *either* of these words, as if it did not matter which, is obviously inaccurate and misleading.

With this necessary distinction well in our minds,

we may turn to the texts in which these words occur. There are two, and only two passages in the Gospels and Epistles in which both one and the other word are employed to translate a Greek word (ἀΐδιος) which unquestionably means "for ever;" and though neither of these texts refers to the future and final conditions of men, we will just glance at them, in order that we may put them aside with a clear conscience, as not bearing on the question in hand. In Romans i. 20, St Paul speaks, according to the Authorized Version, of "the *eternal* power and godhead" of the Almighty; or, as the phrase should be rendered, of "the *everlasting* power and godhead." Now that God's power and deity are everlasting, that they endure for ever, that they can know no bound, no diminution, no end, no man who believes in God at all will be likely to deny. The second passage is Jude 6, where Jude, speaking of the angels who sinned and fell, says that God has reserved them "in *everlasting* chains, under darkness, *unto the day of judgment.*" And here the word is used in a poetic and figurative sense. "Everlasting chains" there may be, though one hardly sees how any "chain" should last for ever; and the fallen angels may be bound by them, though one hardly sees how spirits should be held by chains: but they are not to be bound by them *for ever*, only "*unto the day of judgment.*" All that Jude meant to imply was, therefore, that these fallen spirits were *securely* held, held by bonds they could not hope to break, until the day that should decide their fate. Neither of these passages, then, although they are the only two in which any Greek word is used that, beyond all dispute, signifies " everlasting," at all bears on the question on which we are trying to get a little light.

Laying them aside, then, what have we left? We have this singular and significant fact, that in all the other passages in the Gospels and the Epistles in which the words " eternal " or " everlasting " occur, they are used to translate one Greek word αἰών, and its derivative αἰώνιος,[1]—words which, as I believe I can shew you, so far from denoting either that which is above time, or that which will outlast time, are saturated through and through with the thought and element of time. Now I am sorry to have to trouble you with Greek again; but, you know, it is not my fault that the New Testament was written in Greek : nor can we very well get at the meaning of the Original without studying the Original. At the same time let me say for your encouragement that these two Greek words have been transferred bodily into the English language,

[1] To those who say that though αἰών may or must be taken in a temporal sense, αἰώνιος may or must be taken as having a non-temporal sense—*i.e.*, as meaning either spiritual or everlasting, it should surely be enough to reply that the adjective (αἰώνιος) must derive the *whole* of its meaning from the substantive (αἰών) from which it is derived.

so that even those of you who know nothing of Greek will nevertheless be able to judge what their meaning really is. The Greek word αἰών is simply an earlier form of our word *æon*, which means, as you are aware, an age, an epoch, a period of time which is in some way, from some point of view, a rounded whole, complete in itself. Thus we speak of the æons, or ages, which must have been consumed by the geological changes of the earth, and of the still vaster æons, or ages, necessary for the great astronomical changes that must have preceded the periods during which the void earth was taking its present form. The Greek αἰώνιος, again, is but an earlier form of our word *æonial*, or *æonian*, which means æon-long or age-long; a word not infrequent in our poetry and books of science. When speaking of the immeasurable changes of the natural world, some of our best writers call them " æonial processes " or " æonial changes."

All you need remember is, therefore, that our word *æon*, which means an age, a period, and usually a vast period of time, and our word *æonial*,[1] which means age-long, are not translations of the Greek words αἰών and αἰώνιος, but are the very words themselves bodily lifted out of the one language into the other. Remembering this, you would at once understand what I

---

[1] I retain this as the more familiar form of the word, though *æonian* is the more scholarly and accurate.

meant were I to substitute the Greek words for the words of our Authorized Version in many of the most familiar passages of Scripture. Take, for example, this passage,[1] "Now to the King *eternal*, immortal, invisible, the only wise God, be honour and glory *for ever and ever:* Amen." If I retain the Greek words of which I have spoken, you will quite understand the passage in *this* version of it, though you may not like it so well as the other: "Now to the King *of the æons* (*i.e.*, the King *of the ages*), immortal, invisible, the only wise God, be honour and glory *through the æons of the æons* (*i.e., through the ages of the ages*), Amen." You would understand—and this is precisely what the passage means—that God is here set forth as the King of all the ages of time, and that through all those ages He was to receive honour and glory. But "the King of all the ages of time" is not exactly the same as "the *everlasting* King;" for the ages of time had a beginning and are to have an end: and still less does it convey the idea that would be conveyed by "*eternal* (or spiritual) King," or "King *of eternity*" (*i.e.*, monarch of the spiritual universe).

You see, then, that these words *æon* and *æonial* denote periods, ages of time, however vast, which sooner or later come to a close. And it is very certain that the words were used in this sense by the speakers and

[1] 1 Timothy i. 17.

writers of the New Testament. For, three centuries before the New Testament was first published, the Old Testament was translated from Hebrew into Greek. This translation, the Septuagint, was in common use among the Jews in the time of our Lord. Most of the quotations from the Old Testament which we find in the New were taken from it. It becomes, therefore, an important question for us: In what sense are the words "æon" and "æonial" used in the Septuagint? Do they *there*, and *invariably*, carry either the sense of spirituality of nature or of unending existence? So far from that, these words are commonly and frequently applied to the land promised to the seed of Abraham, which surely was neither an everlasting nor an eternal inheritance; to the Aaronic priesthood, which was not a spiritual priesthood and has already been abolished; to the Temple in Jerusalem, which, long a heap of ruins, is now profaned by "the inexpressible Turk;" to the daily offerings, the "carnal sacrifices," presented in it, which have fallen into disuse for eighteen centuries; and even to the leprosy of Gehazi, which was not a spiritual punishment, and which surely terminated at least at his death.

These are only a few out of a multitude of instances in which the words were applied to places, persons, vocations, accidents which endured only for a time, some of them only for a short time. Of course the words are also and commonly applied to persons and things which *are* spiritual and which *will* endure for ever : to the being of God, for instance, and to the reign of the Messiah. But the question is—and this is the great question we have to determine—do these words, which we admit to be applied to that which is, as well as to that which is not, eternal and everlasting, themselves carry an eternal or everlasting significance ? The answer seems plain. If these words really carried *in themselves* the sense of eternity or of everlastingness, they could not possibly have been applied to that which was so material as the land of Canaan or the Temple at Jerusalem, nor to that which was so transitory as the Levitical functions and offices or as the leprosy of a prophet. Mark this point well, for it is an important one ; words, epithets, could not be applied to that which is carnal or transitory, if in and of themselves they implied in it either a spiritual quality or the quality of endless duration. When, therefore, these words are applied to a Being who is both eternal and everlasting, both spiritual and ever-existing, such as God, or to a reign, the reign of Christ, which is also both spiritual and without end, they cannot fairly be taken as denoting these qualities of spirituality and endlessness in them ; but only as denoting the relation in which God stands to the ages of time, or as affirming that the reign of Christ will extend through all such ages.  The Greek language is not so poor that it cannot convey the idea of spirituality or of unbroken duration in terms not to be mistaken. On the contrary it is even a more precise and flexible language than our own, and contains many words by which it might have conveyed these ideas in the most definite and unquestionable way.  So that when we find the Greek New Testament constantly using the words *æon* and *æonial* where we should have expected to meet words carrying a spiritual or an everlasting significance, we must conclude that these words were used *with intention;* we must also, or at the lowest we may reasonably, conclude that there is hidden in them *some doctrine of the æons,* or ages, which it will repay us to investigate and discover.

Now that there *is* such a doctrine I have more than once pointed out to you when neither you nor I were thinking of the future conditions of men.[1]  Instead of speaking of time as though it were a single period or epoch, the New Testament speaks of it as broken into many ages, in each of which some counsel of the Divine Will is wrought out.  Instead of affirming that time shall be no more when men pass out of this present order and age, it speaks of "ages to come" as well as of "ages that are past."  Thus, for example,

---

[1] The reader, if he cares to look for it, will find a brief statement of this doctrine in *The Expositor,* Vol. iv., pp. 285, *et seq.*

we have, in the past, the age or dispensation prior to the giving of the Law, or the Patriarchal age; then the Mosaic age or dispensation; then the Christian age, or dispensation, of which the Jews spoke familiarly both as " the age of the Messiah " and as " the age to come :" while, in the future, we have apparently many ages, only imperfectly known to us, under such names as the Millennium, the Regeneration, the Restitution of all things, and even ages beyond these which perhaps are all unknown to us. In short, we find in the New Testament a series of æons which are to precede, and in which men are to be prepared for, that final and eternal state in which, Christ having delivered up his Kingdom to the Father, God shall be all in all.

All these preparatory and intermediate ages, moreover, are contained within, are comprehended by, a vast epoch which St Paul calls "*the æon of the æons,*" *i.e.*, the age which includes all ages, which covers the whole course of time; the age also in which what he calls God's "*purpose for the ages,*" *i.e.*, the redemption of the human race, will be wrought out. And how entirely this doctrine falls in with the demands and speculations of modern science and thought you will see at a glance. For *they* demand for the evolution of man, and of the world, and of the universe at large, precisely those past ages and those ages to come of which the New Testament so constantly speaks; and, moreover, *they*, no less emphatically than the New Testament, affirm that all these ages must be gathered up under one, that they must all run up into a sacred unity in which the great scheme or purpose with which universal Nature is pregnant shall be slowly but victoriously developed.

This, stated briefly and in general terms, is the Christian doctrine of the æons, or ages. But as it may be novel, and even startling, to some of you, and as it is the key to all those Scriptures which speak of "*æonial* salvation" and "*æonial* life," or of "*æonial* judgment" and "*æonial* punishment," let me restate it a little more fully.

These æons, or ages, then, as we learn from St Paul, are epochs or periods of time in which God is gradually working out a gracious purpose which He purposed in Christ Jesus long ere man fell from his first estate, long before those "age-times," as he calls them,[1] in and through which men are being recovered from the fall. God's wisdom, he affirms,[2] was "ordained *before the ages* to our glory;" *i.e.*, God, in his wisdom, had determined before time began to educe from the very fall and sin of man a greater glory both to Himself and to us. In his Epistle to the Ephesians[3] he both expressly names God's determination to save men by Christ "*the purpose of the ages*," the end

[1] 2 Timothy i. 9.   [2] 1 Corinthians ii. 7.   [3] Ephesians iii. 11.

that was to be wrought out through all the successions of time; and distinctly asserts that this redeeming work will take "ages" for its accomplishment. In the same Epistle[1] he speaks of the revelation and work of Christ as "the mystery which hath been *hid from the ages*, but is now made manifest;" and of the glory accruing from it to God "*unto all generations of the age of the ages.*" In proof that he anticipates periods after and beyond the Christian era, I cite from this same Epistle[2] the glorious ascription in which he speaks of Christ as set "far above all principalities and powers, and every name that is named, *not only in this age, but in that which is to come;*" and the noble hymn,[3] we might almost call it, in which he sings of the great love wherewith God, who is rich in mercy, hath loved us, quickening us who were dead in sins together with Christ, and raising us together with Him, and establishing us in the heavenly world with Him, "that *in the ages to come* He might shew the exceeding riches of his grace toward us through Christ Jesus." In proof that he conceived of these æons as periods of time which had or would have their commencement and their close, I refer to his description of the believers of his own day[4] as those upon whom "*the ends*

---

[1] Ephesians iii. 9 and 10; 21 (Comp. Colossians i. 26).
[2] *Ibid.*, i. 21.  [3] *Ibid.*, ii. 4-7.  [4] 1 Corinthians x. 11.

*of the ages are met,"*—a phrase which shews that he conceived of the primitive Church as standing at a point at which two great epochs, the Jewish and the Christian, ran together, the terminal end of the one and the initial end of the other meeting, as it were, in the brief span of their single life. And this description is confirmed by a passage in the Epistle to the Hebrews[1] in which it is recorded of Christ, "Now once, *in the end of the ages* (the conclusion or the terminal point, as some take it, *the conjunction* or meeting-point, of the ages, as I take it) He hath appeared to put away sin by the sacrifice of Himself."

For brevity's sake I have as yet only appealed, save in one instance for a confirmation, to the writings of St Paul, although his doctrine of the æons pervades the whole New Testament; but I do not doubt I have already cited passages enough to give you an insight into the meaning and scope of this suggestive but neglected doctrine. I understand him to mean, I understand the New Testament throughout to imply, that, before time began, God foresaw the sin and misery of mankind; that He purposed to redeem us from that sin and misery by the gift and sacrifice of his Son; that the full accomplishment of this great redemptive work, this new creation, will occupy ages to come, just as the creation of the physical universe

[1] Hebrews ix. 26.

has occupied ages that are past ; that the gradual development of this recreative and redeeming purpose is that which binds all the ages of time together in a sacred unity ; and that only when it is carried to its final triumph by the entire redemption of the human race, only when Christ has subdued all things unto Himself, will the successions of time pass away, and God be all in all beings and things, every shadow of evil being swept out of the universe, that the everlasting blessedness of the eternal world may be without spot or stain.

Now if we accept this grand conception of St Paul's, which to my own mind goes far to prove itself by its very grandeur, we hold the key to many of the most difficult passages of Scripture, and especially to those which relate to the life to come. Thus, for example, in Romans xvi. 25 and 26, God Himself is called the *æonial* God. We there read of " the mystery kept secret from *æonial times* (*since the world began*, says the Authorized Version), but which is now made manifest, and by the scriptures of the prophets (*i.e.*, the New Testament prophets, of whom St Paul himself was one), according to the commandment of *the æonial God* (*everlasting* in Authorized Version), is made known to all nations, for the obedience of faith." Now, observe, God is here called " æonial," and certain times are also called " æonial." In both cases, therefore, we must take the epithet in the same sense. But we cannot take the word when it is applied to times or ages, and especially when it is applied to ages that are past, ages in which Jesus Christ was not known, as meaning ceaseless, everlasting; for these ages *have*, long since, *ceased :* and therefore we cannot take it in that sense, when, in the same sentence, it is applied to God. Do we therefore deny that God is eternal and everlasting? By no means. But God is the God of time, as well as the God of eternity. And as St Paul elsewhere attaches epithets to the Divine Name which imply the everlastingness of God, so here he attaches to it an epithet which implies that all the ages of time are under God's control. Was it wrong or misleading to call God "the God of the Jews?" Why, then, should it be wrong or misleading to call Him the God of all men through all the successive periods of the human story down to the very last? No doubt the holy Apostle here speaks of the æonial, rather than of the everlasting, God, because his whole mind was full of that great mystery of love, the purpose of God to redeem the human race by Christ Jesus his Son,—a purpose which, as he believed, it would yet take many ages to accomplish. Of all these ages, he says, God is the God. It is He, the æonial God, who is working in and through them all, and working to bring men, through righteousness, unto life eternal.

So, again, and in like manner, another great Evangelist, the writer of the Epistle to the Hebrews, speaks of Christ[1] as the author of "*æonial* salvation," and [2] as "having obtained *æonial* redemption" for us. Now of course the author of this Epistle, whether Apollos or another, does not mean to deny that the salvation of Christ is an eternal salvation, or that his redemption is an everlasting redemption. In language not to be mistaken he elsewhere implies it to be both everlasting and eternal; but this is not the point which occupies him *here*. He is not teaching that our redemption is a spiritual as opposed to a carnal redemption, or that it will endure for ever. He is rather teaching that it is the redemption proper and peculiar to this Christian age in which we live; that it is the redemption at which Christ laboured while He was with us in the flesh, at which He still labours now that He has gone up on high, and at which He will continue to labour through all those ages to come through which man's appointed course is to run, never lifting his hand from it until the river of time flows into the sea of eternity and is lost in it.

So, once more, in this same Epistle,[3] the Holy Ghost, the Spirit of God and of Christ, is called "the *æonial* Spirit." Not that the writer would for a moment deny this Spirit to be both eternal and

[1] Hebrews v. 9.   [2] *Ibid.*, ix. 12.   [3] *Ibid.*, ix. 14.

everlasting; but he here conceives of Him as the great *Zeit-geist,* or Time-spirit, the Spirit of the Christian age or ages: speaks of Him as animating and informing these ages with a Divine intention and significance, as conducting the whole discipline and culture by which men are led on and up through the successive periods and dispensations of time until they are made perfect in wisdom and righteousness.

And here again we may see how the New Testament, when it is rightly read, not only harmonizes with, but strangely elevates, the highest conceptions of modern thought. Like their German teachers, many of our more advanced English thinkers are for ever speaking of the *Zeit-geist,* the Time-spirit, which broods with quickening heat over the thoughts and aims of men, shaping and conducting them to loftier issues than they had set before themselves, giving to every race or generation its distinctive character and value. To *them* this Time-spirit is a mere abstraction, or it is the final outcome, the general result, of all the best human thinking and acting of the time; an influence generated by the conflicting currents of human thought and endeavour, and, in its turn, generating new currents by which the thoughts and aims of men are swayed. No, says the Scripture; this Zeit-geist, this Time-spirit, is no thin powerless abstraction, no mere blending and sublimation of whatever is best in an age, no unknown power even whose influence is felt, though it itself remains indefinable and unseen. No; there is a Zeit-geist; but this Zeit-geist is a Divine Spirit, the Spirit of God, the Father of all men; the Spirit revealed in Christ, the Saviour of all men. *This* is the Spirit which in very deed sits brooding with wide-extended wings over the successive ages of time; shaping men's thoughts and aims for them, rough-hew them how they will; blending and binding those ages into a sacred unity, and conducting men through them all toward the many mansions of that great House, not made with hands, which is eternal, in the heavens.

Now if you have at all grasped this Christian doctrine of the æons, and of the purpose and work of redemption which is being slowly wrought out in them, you will not be surprised to hear that this same epithet *æonial*, which is applied to God, to Christ, and to the Holy Ghost, is also applied in the New Testament to every particular and aspect of that great redemptive work. If you look back to the Jewish age, you know very well that during that æon a very different, a far inferior, kind of religious life and discipline was open to men as compared with the life and discipline of the present time. If you look forward to the millennial age, whatever your idea of the millennium may be, you expect that men will then enter into a far higher and nobler kind of life than is open to them now, and be trained by a still severer and nobler discipline. And therefore you will expect to hear that the Christian æon has a life and a discipline peculiar to itself. It will not perplex you to read of an "*æonial life*,"[1] or of an "*æonial inheritance*,"[2] in which, by making friends to ourselves of the Mammon of unrighteousness, we may prepare for ourselves "*æonial tents.*"[3] Nor, on the other hand, will it perplex you to read of an "*æonial judgment*,"[4] or an "*æonial punishment*,"[5] or even of an "*æonial fire.*"[6] You will understand that, in the one case, the life that is spoken of as æonial is the life peculiar and proper to these Christian ages, the life of faith in Christ; and that the promised "inheritance" is the happy spiritual estate or condition to which such a life naturally conducts us. And, in the other case, you will readily understand that the æonial judgment is the judgment peculiar to this great series of ages in which God is working out his purpose of redemption; while the æonial fire is a symbol of that æonial punishment which is to be inflicted on all who adjudge themselves unworthy of the life of Christ, the punishment peculiar and proper to the Christian ages. And you will remember that the element and thought of time, of ages, is implied in all these phrases, that it cannot be

---

[1] St John xvii. 3.  [2] Hebrews ix. 15.  [3] St Luke xvi. 9.
[4] St Mark iii. 29.  [5] St Matthew xxv. 46.  [6] Jude 7.

dissociated from aught which pertains to the æons of time; so that even this large and important class of passages does not carry us beyond the bounds of time, and reveals nothing concerning the final and everlasting conditions of men.

All this, however, will, I trust and believe, grow still clearer to you as we proceed, in my next Lecture, to examine more in detail a few of the more important passages in which these words and phrases are employed.

## VI.—THE CHRISTIAN DOCTRINE OF THE ÆONS.

WE have now entered on an investigation of those passages of Scripture in which the future conditions of men are spoken of as eternal and everlasting, with a view to ascertain whether or not they lend any support to the popular conception of a ceaseless torment, an ever-burning hell. To prepare you for a right apprehension of these passages 1 asked you, in my last Lecture, to consider the way in which these words are used in the Bible; and the conclusions we arrived at were such as these. The English words "eternal" and "everlasting" are used to translate the Greek words αἰών and αἰώνιος. Happily these Greek words have been transferred to our own language, so that we can all look at them for ourselves, and in some measure judge what they mean: the Greek αἰών becoming æon in English, and αἰώνιος becoming æonial. Æon, like αἰών, means a term, a period of time, an age, an epoch; and æonial, like αἰώνιος, means that which is of or for an age, that which endures through or pertains unto an epoch of time. So that if we wanted to translate the words æon and æonial, which are mainly used by poets and men of science, into more familiar English, we might very fairly render them by the words *age*, and *age-* or *ages- long*. That the words were used in this sense by the Jews of our Lord's time, that they do not therefore necessarily and invariably imply either spirituality or everlastingness in the objects to which they are applied, I shewed you by alluding to passages in the Greek Version of the Old Testament then in use; passages in which the inheritance of the land of Canaan, the priesthood of the Sons of Aaron, the temple in Jerusalem, the sacrifices offered in it, and even the leprosy of Gehasi, are called *æonial*, though all these were but for a time and have long since come to an end. And to these passages I might have added as many more from the New Testament itself, where the same Greek words are used in precisely the same sense. For there are at least a score of texts in the Scriptures of the New Testament in which these words are confessedly applied to limited periods of time, or to things and persons which were only for a time; as, for example, when St Paul charges them that are rich in this *æon*, or age, that they do not trust in uncertain riches,[1] or as when he complains, "Demas hath forsaken me, having loved this present *æon*."[2]

Beyond a doubt, then, the words *æon* and *æonial* suggest to us an epoch of time, that which is of or for

[1] 1 Timothy vi. 17.     [2] 2 Timothy iv. 10.

an age, or at most that which is for *all* time; and beyond a doubt also they were so used and so understood by our Lord and his Apostles. But were they never used in any other, in any larger sense? That remains to be seen. For the present I simply affirm that, unless some good and sufficient reason for it can be assigned, it cannot be right to translate them by such words as eternal and everlasting; cannot be right to take words which are saturated through and through with the sense of time as though they denoted that which is beyond and above all time. No doubt it was right at one time to translate *æonial* by *eternal*, and would be right again could we reinstate the original significance of the word: for, strangely enough, the word "eternal" originally *meant* æonial or age-long. It comes to us from the Latin *æternus*, the older and longer form of which is *æviternus:* and the word *ævum*, which is the root of it, is simply the Latin form of the Greek αἰών and the English *æon*. But, as we have seen, this word has now come to have two meanings which are as nearly as possible the very opposites of its original meaning. As we now use it, *eternal* means either that which is outside of or above time, or that which outlasts time; that which is spiritual or that which is everlasting. We cannot measure and limit that which is spiritual by the sequences of time; we cannot say that truth is so many years old, or that righteousness and love are so many years long; and therefore we lift them clean out of the inappropriate measures of time, and call them eternal, that is spiritual. And, again, we are quite sure that these august and spiritual realities will outlast all the changes and sequences of time, that they will endure for ever; and therefore we also call them eternal when we really mean that they are everlasting. So that the conclusion at which we arrive is that, since the word "eternal" has so completely changed its meaning, and its meaning is now indeed so indefinite, we must not any longer take it as an equivalent of "æonial." Nay, more: I think we may fairly conclude, as in the last Lecture we did virtually conclude, that since the words in the Original are *æon* and *æonial*, we should always first take them in their first and simplest meaning, as meaning *age* and *age-long*, and see whether we cannot make sense of the passages in which they occur, before we so much as think of looking for any other meaning in them.

And yet, reasonable as it sounds, that is a bold thing to say; for if you turn to any Greek Lexicon, you will find that it gives as the first meaning of αἰών (æon), an age, a period; and almost always gives as an illustration of what it means by an age, the lifetime of a man, the span of human life; but you will also find that it gives as the second meaning eternal, everlasting, and that without assigning any reason whatever for this sudden and stupendous alteration in the value of the word. Now no man likes to contradict the Lexicons. It looks not only bold, but too bold. And when I had done so, I was like Fear in Collin's Ode, ready to recoil at the sound myself had made, for I did not then know that any scholar of repute had adventured himself in this enterprise before me. Judge, then, how welcome a surprise it was when, a few days after the last Lecture had been given, I found all that I had said confirmed and sustained by one who had every right to speak with authority on this point.[1] In reading the Memoir of Charles Kingsley which has just appeared, I lighted on a letter containing these words:

"*The word (αἰών, æon) is never used in Scripture or anywhere else in the sense of endlessness (vulgarly*

---

[1] Whatever may be said of the eagerness and impatience with which Kingsley leaped to his conclusions, and of the tenacity with which he held them, it must be allowed that on subjects within his range and in which he took an interest he was a tolerably accurate observer. He is better known and more commonly thought of as a poet and novelist than as a scholar or divine. But he not only took a first-class in classics at Cambridge, he continued to read the classical authors with delight to the day of his death. The "fathers" of the Church were familiar to him, as Hypatia will avouch. And when his friend and "master" Maurice was compelled to withdraw from King's College mainly for denying the endless torment dogma, Kingsley made a special study of this question of the future conditions of human life, and continued to brood over it for many years. I take his word on such a point as this to be worth much, therefore.

*called eternity*). *It always meant, both in Scripture and out, a period of time.* Else how could it have a *plural*—how could you talk of *the* æons, and æons of æons, as the Scripture does? Nay, more, how talk of οὗτος ὁ αἰών (this age), which the translators, with laudable inconsistency, have translated 'this world,' *i.e.*, this present state of things, age, dispensation, or epoch. Αἰώνιος (æonial) *therefore means, and must mean, belonging to an epoch, or the epoch;* and αἰώνιος κόλασις (æonial punishment) is the punishment allotted to that epoch."[1]

But I need not say more on the meaning of the words *æon* and *æonial*. You have now, besides your own common sense, high authority for believing that they do not imply endlessness whether in Scripture or

[1] Since meeting these words of Kingsley's, which confirm my position point by point, I have found that Dr Abbott, the head master of the City of London School—a scholar himself and a very efficient cause of scholarship in others—leans to, probably holds, the same conclusion. For, in his "Cambridge Sermons" (page 25), he writes: "And as for ourselves, though occasionally mentioning, in language general and metaphorical, *states of æonian life and æonian chastisement* awaiting us after death, the Holy Scriptures give no detailed information as to either condition." No competent English writer would have spoken of *æonian* life and *æonian* punishment, if he believed the commoner phrases, such as "eternal life" and "everlasting punishment," would have as accurately conveyed his meaning.

Since the above Note was written Dr Abbott has put this point beyond doubt. In his very thoughtful book, "Through Nature to Christ," he expressly affirms his conviction that the received dogma is untenable, and falls back both on the interpretation and the conclusion for which I am contending.

out of it; that they always carry in them the suggestion of periods and epochs of time. Let us at once turn, therefore, to some crucial passages in the New Testament, examine them in the light of this hypothesis, and see whether we can make good sense of them.

There is, however, a large and important class of passages at which we must glance, those in which *æonial life* is mentioned or defined, before we pass on to the more difficult and decisive passages which speak of æonial judgment or æonial punishment. You will all remember such passages as that in which the Young Lawyer asks, "What shall I do that I may inherit æonial life?" or that in which our Lord bids the Jews, "Search the Scriptures, since in them ye think ye have æonial life, and these are they which testify of me;" or that in which He affirms, "Whosoever believeth in the Son of Man shall not perish, but have life æonial;" or that in which He gives the definition, "This is æonial life, that they might know Thee, the only true God, and Jesus Christ whom Thou hast sent." And if we put away from ourselves for a moment the thoughts and associations which naturally cluster round these passages for us, and try to read them in the sense in which the Jews who first heard them would take them, is it difficult to understand that they all refer, and were understood to refer, to that life which is proper and peculiar to the Christian age or dispensation? Need we import our ideas of "eternal" and "everlasting" into them? Can we import these ideas into them without so far forth departing from the sense in which they were then apprehended? The Jews were quite familiar with this doctrine of the ages. They knew very well that the age of Moses was to be succeeded by the age of the Messiah, that the Legal was to be followed by the Christian dispensation. They spoke familiarly of the former as "the age that now is," and of the latter as "the coming age:" and they were quite aware that the religious life of the coming age, the age of the Christ, would be both higher and broader than the life proper to the Legal age, that it would be something more and better than a life of obedience to national laws and carnal commandments. What more natural, then, than that when the Messiah came they should ask Him what they must do in order to rise into this new and higher life, what new and greater commandments they must keep in order to lay hold of the life proper to the age of the Messiah? What more natural than that He should refer them to their own Scriptures as containing hints and predictions of what this new life should be, and affirm that these Scriptures bore witness to the very kind of life they might find in Him? What more natural than that He should assert, "Whosoever believeth in me shall not perish," *i.e.*, shall not find his old religious life come to an end, but, on the contrary, shall find it rise and expand into the new better life proper to this new age ? How could He more exactly define this new life than by telling them that henceforth they must not only believe in the only true God—this belief in one only and true God having always been the distinctive creed of the Jew and the source of his distinctive spiritual life ; but must also believe in *Him*, the Christ, whom at last that God had sent to save and bless them, as He had promised to their fathers ? How could they possibly rise into the new life, the distinctively Christian life, except by faith in the Christ ?

Surely, then, this much is clear,—that we are not driven to put our ideas of "eternal" and "everlasting" into this large and important class of passages. We can make perfectly good sense of them, and I am bold to add a sense much more clearly historical and appropriate, by taking æonial life to mean the special and distinctive life of the Christian æons, that form of spiritual life which came with Christ, which is to endure through all the Christian ages, and which will probably be succeeded by still higher and more heavenly forms of life when the redemption of Christ shall be fully accomplished.

But will the same interpretation hold equally good

of the passages in which an *æonial death and punishment* are denounced against the wicked. Let us see.

Turn first to Jude 7. In Verse 6 there is a passage we have already considered.[1] Jude there says that the angels who sinned and fell are reserved in everlasting chains, *i.e.*, are securely bound, "unto the day of judgment," when of course they are to be released from their chains, and judged by God—perchance to be restored to their first estate if they have repented while "in prison," perchance to be condemned to "some worse thing" should they have remained impenitent. In any case their fate is not yet fixed for ever. There is still a "judgment" before them. In Verse 7 Jude illustrates their doom by that of the cities of Sodom and Gomorrha, cities which our Lord Himself assures us "*would* long ago have repented" had they seen his works. For their sins, however, they are "set forth as an example, suffering (not the vengeance of eternal fire, as the Authorized Version has it, but) *the sentence of æonial fire*." Now if we take this æonial fire to signify the punishment inflicted on unrepented sins during a certain age, or certain ages, of time, we not only get a perfectly good sense out of the words, a sense in harmony with the general teaching of the New Testament, but the very sense which this passage taken as a whole imperatively

[1] See page 99.

demands. For the doom of Sodom and Gomorrha is introduced with an ὡς (even as), and is obviously intended as a parallel to, an illustration of, the doom which fell on the sinful angels. Can it then be a worse, a more enduring, doom than theirs? What becomes of the parallel if it is? Yet the sinful angels are only doomed "until the day of judgment." The sinful Cities of the Plain, therefore, are only doomed until that day. Before *them* there is still a judgment. At this judgment their case will be reconsidered. A new sentence may be pronounced on them. And if, while they were "spirits in prison" they saw Christ and his works, as St Peter implies that all the spirits in prison did when Christ descended into Hades, then, according to our Lord's words, they have "long ago repented": and who can doubt that their repentance will be unto life? There is good reason, therefore, to hope that even the men of Sodom and Gomorrha, like the disobedient generation of Noah,[1] have been saved, or will be saved; that, though doomed for an age to the æonial fire which alone could burn out their sins, they will no longer be adjudged unworthy of eternal life on the great day of account.

In 2 Thessalonians i. 9, a new phrase, a new conception, meets us. St Paul affirms that those who knew not God, though they might have known Him,

[1] 1 Peter iii. 20.

and did not obey the Gospel of Christ, although they heard it, " shall be punished with *æonial destruction* from the presence of the Lord and from the glory of his power," on some day when Christ will come to be glorified in his saints and to be wondered at in all them that believe. On what day this revelation of Christ is to take place we cannot tell and need not speculate. The Greek formula which St Paul employs, as even the most straitly orthodox, as even the hyper-orthodox admit, denotes " some single point of time distinct from the actual present, but the exact epoch of which is left uncertain." [1] But assuredly the Apostle gives us no hint that he is thinking of *the end* of time. Rather his general course of thought implies that he is speaking of the very men who then troubled and persecuted the Thessalonian Converts to the Christian Faith ; and threatening them that, *for the age which is to commence with their condemnation*, they shall not be permitted to behold the glory and triumph of Christ. *Æonial* destruction ought to mean *age-long* destruction, as we have seen : and an age-long destruction from the presence and glory of Christ, *i.e.,* the being shut out from all sight of and participation in the triumphs of Christ during that age, appears to be, so far as we can recover it, the very thought St Paul had in his mind. Just as we are told that there

[1] Bishop Ellicott *in loco.*

are some men who will not have part in the first resurrection, but will have part in the general resurrection of the dead; so also there are some who for their sins will be debarred from the presence and glory of Christ for an age, the age perhaps which immediately succeeds this present life, and yet abide in his presence and share his glory in the ages beyond. At all events such an interpretation makes perfectly good sense of the passage; it is the natural and common sense interpretation of the words; it does not, like the commonly received interpretation, shock the reason and natural sense of justice of every unprejudiced mind: why then should we cast about for another?

But let us turn to more decisive passages than these. In St Matthew xviii. 8 and 9, we have a passage on which I had to speak[1] when dealing with the New Testament use of the word "Hell." But as it is one of the great proof-texts with those who uphold the popular dogma, and as moreover the word translated "eternal" and "everlasting" occurs in it, as well as the word "hell," we must look at it again. Our Lord here counsels us that if hand or foot offend us, we should cut them off, lest (verse 8) we be "cast into *the æonial fire.*" In Verse 9 He once more bids us rule and deny our strongest cravings, lest we be cast into "*the Gehenna of fire.*" The two phrases, "æonial

[1] See page 83.

fire" and "the Gehenna of fire," are equivalents, you see; they both point to the same terrible doom. But we have ascertained what one of them means. We have seen that "the Gehenna of fire," so far from indicating the final and endless condition of the wicked, indicates only an intermediate and temporary condition; their condition in that dim Hadean world in which the wicked are afflicted, tormented, and perchance led to repentance and life, before the great and terrible day of the Lord come. And as "æonial fire" is equivalent to, as it is only another way of saying, "Gehenna of fire," we have in this passage a clear proof that æonial means, not everlasting, but age-long,—one such clear and convincing proof outweighing, remember, any number of dubious hints or probable arguments. Just as in this great Christian epoch there is a life which is proper to it and distinctive of it, so also are there a death, a fire, a judgment, a destruction, a punishment which are also proper to it and distinctive of it: and these, like the "life," are called *æonial* to mark the fact that they belong to the Christian age and are peculiar to it.

This passage of St Matthew's is reported at still greater length by St Mark (ix. 42-50); and in this form it is one of the most solemn and terrible utterances of our Lord. The iterations and reiterations in it are simply appalling. The æonial fire of Gehenna, that doleful region of the nether-world, "where their worm dieth not, and the fire is not quenched," is brought before us again and again. No passage is more frequently cited by those who believe in what Shakspeare calls "th' everlasting bonfire." And therefore, though I must go a little out of the way to do it, let me say a few words on its ruling conceptions and images. I have already explained its technical phrases. I have shewn you that the Jewish prophets and apostles, even our Lord Himself, took the imagery of the passage—the undying worm and the unquenchable fire—from that detestable valley of Ge hinnom outside the walls of Jerusalem where the fire and the worm were for ever at work on the refuse of the city. I have told you in what sense the Jews of our Lord's time understood these figures when they were used *as* figures of speech; how they believed that the incorrigibly wicked would be subjected to searching torments for a brief space of time, and then either be reclaimed by the mercy of God or destroyed by his mighty power. And now I have only to ask you to put out of your thoughts for a moment all the interpretations put upon the passage by those fathers and inquisitors of the Church who did not hesitate to consign the bodies of men to the torments of a slow fire, and who naturally enough created a God after their own image, a God who, as we read in Boston's *Fourfold State,* would "hold up the wicked in hell-fire with the one hand, and torment them with the other." Put all these morbid horrors clean out of your minds; if you will, put all true, as well as these untrue, historical interpretations out of your minds; and then come to these terrible words with the wind of healthy common sense blowing about you, and look at them for yourselves.

Perhaps the very first thing that strikes you is, that even the bold cruel men who adopted, and formulated, and to whom we are mainly indebted for the current libel on God, have played fast and loose with their own favourite scriptures. Our Lord speaks of the worm that dieth not, as well as of the fire that is not quenched. But they, though they are sure the fire is a real fire, are not so sure that the worm is a real worm. They have not scrupled to depict the future world of the wicked as an enormous furnace, in which the souls of men writhe in intolerable and hopeless agonies for ever and for ever; but even they have not dared to paint *a world all worm,* a world in which the souls of men are exposed to the various and sickening horrors of corruption. Why? Simply, I believe, because they felt that superstition itself would have recoiled before such horrors as these, and have refused to believe that such a world as *that* could possibly have been the handiwork of God; or because even they themselves consciously or unconsciously revolted from a conception so coarse and horrible. Yet our Lord speaks of the worm just as emphatically as He speaks of the fire. And if men cannot believe in a world all worm, why should they believe in a world all fire?

But consider again: when our Lord speaks of the worm and the fire, we must take Him to mean either the actual worm and the actual fire of the Gehenna valley, or some spiritual analogue of these, some discipline, some torment, which effects in the spiritual world what the real worm and the real fire do in the natural world. Go to the natural world, then, and ask what are the functions of the worm and the fire. The function of worms in the natural world is to prevent, though they seem to promote, putrefaction. They feed on the noxious matter which would else breed infection; they transmute the refuse of decay into their own living and healthy organisms. Fire, again, consumes dead and noxious matter, leaving only the ash, which is the best manure of a new crop, transmuting all else into higher and invisible forms. To rid the earth of that which is noxious and infectious, to transmute it into vital and wholesome forms—this is the proper function of both worm and fire in the natural world. What then can the moral analogue of them be but a discipline so searching, so severe, as that it shall destroy that which is corrupt and corrupting, render innoxious that which is noxious, and evolve life itself from the very jaws of death ?[1]

Does not Nature itself, then, teach us all, and more than all, that we have learned from language and history of the true meaning of our Lord's words ?

If even the voice of Nature does not suffice, let Christ be his own interpreter. As this solemn passage draws to a close, He utters words (verse 49) which clearly indicate what He meant by threatening the corruptions bred in us by self-indulgence with æonial fire: "For *everyone* shall be salted with fire." The allusion is of course to the sacrifices offered in the Jewish Temple. These were salted with salt—the salt being an emblem of the life and purification wrought in the conscience of the offerer when they were duly presented. In like manner, our Lord teaches, every soul of man, who is to become an acceptable offering unto God, will and must be salted with fire, *i.e.*, exposed to a still more searching, purify-

---

[1] "When Christ says, Better life with self-mortification than self-indulgence with Gehenna, Gehenna on his tongue must needs stand for *corruption*, since corruption is the antithesis of life, and the literal Gehenna, as we have seen, was emphatically *the place of corruption*. . . . . For what were the fires of Gehenna lighted? To inflict pain and anguish? No; but to get rid of the city's impurity. All its various filth was there: and for what purpose? That by the action of fire it might be licked up and purged away. The flame of the valley of Hinnom cannot be made to represent the awful *suffering* in store for sin: it can only fitly represent the certain *consumption* of sin, to be effected through the *sharpness* of fire."—*Echoes of Spoken Words.* By S. A. Tipple.

ing, and quickening element than salt—to a discipline still more severe and penetrating. As to the time when this discipline will be granted or inflicted our Lord is silent. But obviously He means that at some time every man, who is to be redeemed, must pass through it. We may inflict it on ourselves here and now if we will, voluntarily passing through the fire of self-denial and self-restraint: but if we shrink from this fire, then hereafter, when we have grown at once more weak and more corrupt by habits of self-indulgence and self-will, a fiercer and more penetrating fire of remorse and shame and punishment will be kindled within us. But in one way or the other, in this age or in the ages to come, our sins, the sins of every one of us, must be burned out. Here, then, our Lord explains his own thought to us, and shews us that the fire of Gehenna, the æonial fire, which He had in view was the symbol not of a vindictive and degrading punishment, but of a purifying and vivifying correction. "Our God is a consuming fire;" and a fire that will burn on until all that is evil is burned up.

St Mark (iii. 29) reports other words spoken by Christ which have carried fear and dismay into many an honest and good heart, but which we are now in a position to understand in their true sense. How many, alas, have fancied, how many have persuaded themselves, that they had committed the sin against the Holy Ghost! how many even have been driven by the consequent fear of hell into asylums many of which were, in past days, veritable hells! And yet, now that we apprehend what the words *æon* and *æonial* mean, how easy it is to take all that power of inspiring abject terror and hopeless despair out of them! I need do little more than read them to you in the light of what you have already heard. "But he that shall blaspheme against the Holy Ghost is not to be forgiven in this *æon*, but is in danger of *æonial* judgment." A man may blaspheme the God who speaks to him from without, in the person or by the representatives of the Son of Man, and be forgiven even in this present age; but the man who blasphemes against the God within him, the Holy Ghost—the man who calls that right which he knows and feels to be wrong, and who, knowing the good, deliberately says to evil, "Be thou *my* good," is not to be forgiven in this age. No, verily: for this age has brought him all that it has to bring, and he has rejected it: the most penetrating and intimate ministries of Divine Grace have been vouchsafed him, and he has resisted them: let him feel *the judgments* of this age, since he will not accept its choicest gifts; let him pass out of this age only to enter into the discipline of the next: and as he suffers these æonial judgments, let him consider and reconsider himself, lest he also lose the ages beyond.

There is but one other passage to which I need refer you. It is the great passage recorded in St Matthew xxv. 31-46. And here you must observe that the passage is *a parable;* and that the parable is concerning *nations,* not individual men, as our Lord Himself tells us at the very outset (verse 32): "And before Him shall be gathered *all nations,* and He shall separate them one from another, as a shepherd divideth his sheep from his goats." You must also remember, if you intend to found any conclusion on the parable, or to infer from words spoken of nations conclusions which touch the lot and fate of individual men, that the Judge is here set forth in the tender and familiar form of a Shepherd; that to the Eastern shepherd his goats are well-nigh, if not quite, as dear as his sheep: and that the left hand of a Judge or Ruler is the next best place to his right hand. Nay, more, you must mark—and this is a point which does not appear in our Authorized Version—that our Lord speaks in a certain gentle and kindly, even in a pitiful and caressing tone, of those who are ranged on the left hand of the Judge. The words he uses for them is not "goats." In Verse 32, he speaks of the Shepherd as dividing his sheep, not from his goats, but from his "*kids;*" and in Verse 33, He takes a still tenderer tone, and speaks of the Shepherd-Judge as setting his sheep on his right hand, but his "*kidlings*"—a diminutive of kids, and, like all such diminutives, an expression of affection—on his left.

These considerations, these hints of mercy and compassion, may well make us careful as to the conclusions we deduce from this great passage. And even when the veil of Parable falls aside, and we seem to get clear and distinct statements, at least on the fate of nations, if not on that of their individual units, we have still to remember that the Judge is depicted as rendering to every one the due reward of his deeds, and of *all* his deeds. It is implied that if any one has so much as given a cup of cold water to the least of Christ's brethren, he, though himself not a brother, shall in no wise lose his reward.

And, finally, we have to examine the terms in which these future rewards are expressed. To those who stand on his left hand the Judge is represented as saying, "Depart from me, ye cursed of my Father, *into the æonial fire*." Now I have no wish to abate the impressive sadness, the awful severity, of these words. "The wrath of the Lamb" of God *must* be very terrible. And to hear Him whose gracious lips have always hitherto said, "Come unto me," say "Depart from me," will be an experience so sad, a surprise so terrible, as that I can well believe every man who hears that rebuff from his meek and gracious lips will wish that he had never been born; yes, and wish he had never been born even though he understands that he is banished from the presence of Christ *only for an age*, only that the age-long fire may consume his sins and burn out his unrighteousness. But to say that those who have rejected Christ in this present age are to be doomed to an *everlasting* banishment from his mercy is to contradict Christ Himself, who expressly tells us[1] that all manner of blasphemy against the Son of Man may be forgiven both in this age *and in that which is to come*. And, moreover, it is to import a new meaning into the word "æonial," which, as we have seen, means "age-long," and to import it quite unnecessarily, since if we take our Lord as meaning that our rejection of Him in this age will be punished by banishment from Him in the age to come, we find a very good and a sufficient sense in his words; whereas if we take Him as meaning that to reject Him in this brief life is to be excluded from his love for ever, we not only strike a note utterly discordant with the tender and pitiful tone in which He speaks throughout the Parable, but we also introduce that vast, unreasonable, unjust disproportion between our deeds here and their results hereafter from which Reason and Conscience alike revolt.

But what are we to say to the closing words (*verse* 46) of the Parable? "These shall go away into

[1] St Matthew xii. 31, 32.

*æonial* punishment, but the righteous into life *æonial.*" Well, we may say this. Take the phrase "æonial life" to mean here, as elsewhere, life in Christ, the spiritual life distinctive of the Christian æons, and "æonial punishment" to mean here, as elsewhere, the discipline, the punishment distinctive of the Christian æons, the punishment which those inflict on themselves who adjudge themselves unworthy of that life, and the words make a very good and reasonable sense, a sense so reasonable that we need search for no other. And mark, in *this* case at least, we cannot put a darker sense into the words of Christ except by trifling with them, and implying that we know what He meant better than He did Himself. For the word here rendered "punishment" (κόλασις) is a very peculiar one. In its primary use, when it is applied to natural processes, it means "*pruning,*" *i.e.*, pruning bushes and trees in order that they may bring forth more fruit. When it is used figuratively, when it is applied to moral processes, it means corrective discipline, discipline by which character is pruned and made more fruitful in good works. The Greek has two words for "punishment;" κόλασις, the word used by our Lord, and τιμωρία, a word also used in the New Testament (Heb. x. 29): and the distinctive meanings of these two words are defined by Aristotle himself.[1]

[1] *Rhet.* I., 10, 17.

The one word, that used by Christ, denotes, he says, that kind of punishment which is intended for the improvement of the offender; while the other denotes that kind of punishment which is intended for the vindication of law and justice. And even the advocates of endless torment admit that the word selected by Christ means, according to the Greek usage, remedial discipline, punishment designed to reform and improve men, to prune away their defects and sins. Archbishop Trench,[1] for example, after adverting to the well-known distinction between the two words κόλασις and τιμωρία, confesses that while the latter is used to indicate "the vindicative character of punishment, the former indicates punishment as it has reference to *the correction and bettering* of the offender." And I do not know where we shall find a sadder instance of the way in which good men suffer their theories and traditions to warp their judgment than may be found in the fact that, after thus defining the original and proper sense of the word used by Christ, this good and learned man proceeds to say that it would however be "a very serious error" to take the word in its proper sense here. We, on the contrary, maintain that it would be something worse than an error to take it in any but its usual and proper sense. And, therefore, we conclude that our Lord meant precisely what He

[1] Synonyms of the New Testament, pp. 23, 24.

said; viz., that the wicked should go away from his bar to be pruned, go away into an age-long discipline by which they should be castigated for their sins, yea, and saved from their sins by the corrective discipline of his loving wrath. For that would not be a corrective discipline which left men unimproved for ever; that would be a strange sort of "pruning," which was not at least designed to produce fruit.

"O, but," say some, who little think what they are saying, "*the same word* is here used of the life promised to the righteous which is used of the punishment of the unrighteous; each is called *æonial*: and if the punishment of the wicked is not to last for ever, what guarantee have we that the felicity of the good, *our* felicity, will last for ever?" To that question I reply by another. Would you, then, have the vast majority of men damned to an everlasting torture in order that you may feel quite sure that your timid soul will "sit and sing itself away in everlasting bliss?" If your soul is capable of no higher flight than that, is it worth saving? is it capable of everlasting bliss? Moses could wish himself blotted from the book of life, St Paul could wish himself "anathema" from Christ, so that Israel, their brethren according to the flesh, might be saved. And Christ both could and did far more than wish; He, who knew no sin, became sin for us, that we might be made the righteousness of

God in Him. And He Himself has taught us that he who would save his soul must be willing to lose his soul. How much of his spirit can we have, then, if, instead of wishing ourselves damned for the sake of the world, we are willing that the world should be damned for the sake of our timorous and foreboding souls?

My friends, if we love Christ, we need have no fear for our souls. In sundry places and in terms not to be mistaken, all who trust in Him are assured of an eternal salvation, a life that can never die. But if we truly love Him, we are willing even to die in order that the world may be saved: for did not *He* die to take away the sin of the world? and must not we be made partakers of his death, if we are to be glorified together with Him? Unless I can believe that God will deign to use me for the good of others, what is my life worth to me? Not to be capable of living and suffering for others, *that* is the true hell; but to be capable of, to be allowed to serve and suffer for others, is the true heaven: for this is the very life of God Himself, and of Christ Jesus his Son, and of the ever-blessed ever-quickening Spirit.

## VII.—THE TEST AND THE TESTIMONY OF PRINCIPLES.

IT is not reasonable to expect that, while we are in this chrysalis and initial stage of our being, we should be able to comprehend what the final stage of our career will be like, if indeed there can be a *final* condition to finite creatures who are to live, and to grow, for ever, and who must therefore, one should think, be ever reaching forth to that which is before and above them. And accordingly, as we have seen, Holy Scripture does not profess or attempt to disclose the secrets of the remote future, but only to give us some general indications of what our several conditions will be in the stages and æons which immediately succeed to the present life. Nay, more, however deeply we may long for it, and however full and varied the Scripture revelation concerning it may be, or may seem to be, it is not possible that we, who reach even our most immaterial conception through the gates and avenues of sense, should be able to formulate any complete and accurate theory of the life to come, the life which is independent of the senses, even though it be still within the compass of time. But we may hope, by a careful examination of those scriptures which are held to support the current theory of that life to shew that, so far from supporting, they contradict and disprove it; and we may also hope to shew that great principles, what we call "doctrines," which are wrought into the very substance of Scripture and pervade it from end to end, point in an entirely opposite direction, and render the current theory altogether untenable. And this is the task which we have set ourselves to attempt.[1]

Now in so far as the future condition of the wicked is concerned, we have already discharged the more difficult and tedious part of our task. We have examined the scriptures on which the popular conception rests; and we have found that they lend no support to the notion that the wicked and impenitent, from the very moment they pass out of this life, are damned to hell, *i.e.*, doomed to an endless and unredeeming torment. I have shewn you that the verb "to damn" should be expunged from the New Testament, since the Greek verbs rendered by it commonly mean only "to judge," and never mean more than "to condemn." I have shewn you that the substantive "hell" should also be expunged from the New Testament, since it is used to translate the Greek nouns "Tartarus," "Hades," "Gehenna," and these words point, not to a final and endless state of torture,

---

[1] See Lecture II., pages 31 *et seq.*

but to an intermediate and temporal state of discipline which reaches at the farthest only to "the day of judgment." And I have shewn you that the Greek and English adjective "æonial," which is commonly translated by "eternal" or "everlasting," means no more than "age-long," and points, when used of the future, to the age or dispensation which is to succeed the dispensation in which we now live, an age which has a life, a reward, a bliss peculiar to itself, and also a death, a pruning, a discipline peculiar to itself.

The way we have traversed has been long and often tedious, for we have had to study somewhat minutely a large number of texts; but the conclusion we have reached is, I trust, one in which we can rest all the more securely because of the pains we have taken to reach it. For, you will observe, our conclusion is but one, though it has taken many forms, and though it has been drawn from many passages of Holy Writ. And our conclusion is this: In an immense variety of ways the New Testament teaches us to believe that men who die in their sins will be adjudged to a state in which, for an age, or for ages if need be, they will be exposed to a corrective discipline far more searching and severe than that to which they are exposed now, and by which we may hope they will be recovered to righteousness and life. And if it is satisfactory, if it strengthen our faith in our conclusion, to have been led up to it by so many different lines of thought, by scriptures so numerous and so various, it should still further assure our hearts to find that the conclusion to which we have been led by our study of Scripture is one which our reason approves and our sense of justice. Do what we will, we cannot make it seem fair and reasonable that a God of perfect justice and perfect goodness should doom men to a torture which has no end, which will do nothing to correct or amend them; that He will keep them alive for ever in agonies which will only harden and degrade them for sins committed in these brief hours of time, on the spur of a nature already depraved when they received it, and at the solicitation of external influences and conditions which they did not charge with their power to tempt and allure to evil, and from which they cannot possibly discharge that power. But, on the other hand, is it not most fair and reasonable that men who have had no chance of life here should have one hereafter; that those who have thrown away their chance should suffer for it in the age to come, and so suffer as to be taught their folly and their sin before a final sentence, if indeed any such sentence can be final, be pronounced upon them?

Now till we had examined in some detail the passages from which the popular conception is drawn, it would have been of little use for me to speak of those great pervading principles, or doctrines, which are inconsistent with it. You would have been for ever recalling this text or that which seemed to contradict the conclusion to which you were being led. But now that we have examined them, and have done our best to discover what they really mean, I trust you will be able to turn to a consideration of these principles with an open and untroubled mind.

For myself I am glad that this necessary, yet less welcome and less conclusive, part of our task is over, and that we may pass on and up from these minute critical investigations to breathe a larger air and to move freely along a higher path. For not only does it cramp and deaden the spirit that is in man to tarry long in the low valley of mere criticism, where the atmosphere is commonly charged with the elements of polemical strife; but it is also impossible for him, until he climb up out of it, to gain any broad, decisive, and inspiring view of the truth for which he contends. For no conclusion can be safely based on the study of scattered and isolated texts. It is the Bible, alas! of which it has been written,

> "This is the book where each his own dogma seeks;
> And this the book where each his own dogma finds."

Even with our best care, and the sincerest endeavour to deal honestly both with ourselves and the Bible, it is difficult, if not impossible, to escape the bias of our own nature and preconceptions; it is difficult even to avoid selecting those texts which support the view to which we lean, and twisting in our own favour those which tell against us. I can claim, indeed, to have aimed at handling the Word of God sincerely throughout this discussion; but I do not therefore infer that I have succeeded in escaping my own natural bent. I frankly admit that another man as sincere as I, and far more competent, in his search of the Scriptures might have lit on quite another series of passages to that which I have asked you to consider. I frankly concede even that, had he selected the same passages, he might have put another, and not wholly unreasonable, interpretation upon them. All I can plead for my selection is that I have not made it for myself; it has been made for me by those who hold other views than mine, and is constantly adduced in support of their views. All I can plead for my interpretation, beyond honesty of intention, is, that *all* these passages, thus interpreted, seem to run up easily and fairly into one and the same conclusion, and that this conclusion accords with the plain dictates of reason and the moral sense. But if, now that we have put our interpretation upon them and reached our conclusion, we bring that conclusion to the test of the great leading principles which confessedly pervade the whole Bible, and find that they will stand *this* test, then I think we may safely infer that our method of interpretation is a true one, and our conclusion one on which we may rely. It is with a great sense of relief, therefore, for I have no fear as to the issue of the experiment, that, leaving the discussion of isolated texts, I ask you to turn to a consideration of large and accepted doctrines, in order that you may put our conclusion to this crucial and decisive test.

(1.) Take, first, *the doctrine of Retribution.* Throughout the Bible we are taught that both in this world and in that which is to come every man receives, or will receive, according to his works or deeds,—'according to that he hath done, whether it be good or whether it be bad.' 'Whatsoever a man soweth, that shall he also reap' is the familiar illustration of this principle, or law, both in the Old Testament and in the New. Perhaps Jeremiah[1] gives it the noblest expression in the words, 'I, the Lord, search the heart, I try the reins, *to give every man according to his ways, according to the fruit of his own doings.*' But I need not cite texts in proof that this Law of Retribution *is* a law

---

[1] The passage will be found in Jeremiah xvii. 10. As a proof of the constant iteration and reiteration of this principle in the Bible I may mention that any one who will turn up the word 'according' in a Concordance will find the following references to passages in which it is enunciated, which of course are not a tithe of the places in which it is really taught and illustrated : Job xxxiv. 11 ; Psalm lxii. 12 ; Prov. xxiv. 12 ; Jer. xxi. 14, and xxxii. 19 ; St Matt. xvi. 27 ; Rom. ii. 6 ; 2 Cor. v. 10, Rev. ii. 23 ; xx. 12, 13, and xxii. 12.

both of this life and of the next; for I am sure you instantly recognize it as a law revealed both in the Divine Providence which controls the lives of men and nations, and in the Word of Inspiration.

But of this Law we are apt to frame very partial and misleading conceptions. We are apt to assume that Retribution means only that the bad man will be punished and the good man rewarded,—as if all men were either wholly good or wholly bad! We forget the complexities of human character, and the consequent complexity of the recompences which await us; and thus we create many difficulties for ourselves even as we study the history and fate of men in this present world. Who has not been puzzled and perplexed, for example, when considering the story of Esau and Jacob, at finding that while *our* sympathy instinctively goes out toward the bold impetuous hunter, *God's* sympathy and goodwill seem to go out toward the timid and crafty shepherd? What profound and far-reaching solutions of this problem have been propounded when, but for our partial conceptions of the law of Retribution, there would absolutely be no problem to solve! Esau *was* bold and impetuous; he loved hunting, loved power over men, loved immediate gratification and visible success. And he had his reward. He enjoyed the adventurous life of the hunter and the conqueror; he became a "duke" or leader of men, and was established in the fastnesses of Edom. But, at the best, was he much more than a type of that "healthy animalism" as we call it, which has gone far, despite our admiration of it, to ruin the world? Was he nothing but bold and generous? Was he not also careless, reckless, self-regarding, worldly, unspiritual? Would it have been just, then, to bestow on him, not only the appropriate rewards of his good qualities, but also a reward which his evil qualities and defects incapacitated him to receive? Would it have been of any use even, would it have been of any comfort or pleasure to him, to bestow on him the spiritual gifts for which he had no capacity; to send him visions he could not see, and voices he could not hear, and thus to call him to a life of faith and self-sacrifice? Such a summons would have simply been intolerable to him, he being what he was; and the mere attempt, had he even made the attempt, to grasp and respond to it would have been as distasteful to him as ineffective. On the other hand, Jacob *was* crafty and mean, and was punished for it all his life long. Cheated and betrayed by Laban, by his wives, by his sons, and, worst of all, in the person of Joseph " whom he loved more than all his sons," he had to eat the bitter fruit of his own doings. But was Jacob nothing but crafty and mean? Could he not value and prefer the future to the present, the spiritual to the sensual? Was not the birthright which Esau "despised," unspeakably precious to him? And if it was just that he should be chastised for his meanness and subtlety, was it not also just that he should be rewarded for his spirituality, that he should receive the visions for which he had an eye, the oracles for which he had an ear, and the training by which he had the heart to profit?

You see, the very moment we look at the whole man, and apply the Law of Retribution through the whole circle of his qualities, capacities, deeds, the dealing of God with Esau and Jacob is strictly and conspicuously just. But this same Law, as the Scriptures emphatically declare, is to govern the awards of the life to come as well as the events of the life that now is. And if, instead of taking part of the law and applying it to part of a man, we take the whole law and apply it to the whole man, what room do we leave for the everlasting damnation of the wicked, or indeed for the immediate and perfect felicity of the just? For even the best of men carries out of this world some taints of evil, and many lingering traces of imperfection. And even the worst of men is not wholly bad, not so bad but that he has done some kind deeds, or cherishes some unselfish affection. Is the good man, then, to receive the due reward of his good deeds, but no reward—no punishment, no discipline

—for his bad deeds and for the evil that still cleaves to him and needs to be purged out of him? And the bad man, is he to get the due reward of his bad deeds, but no reward for his good deeds, no training for his good and pure affections? Is God to deal with us in the next world, as He dealt with Esau and Jacob in this world, meting out to each of them the exact reward of his deeds, both good and bad, and graciously adding to each the very discipline he required in order that the most and the best might be made of him? Or is God to deal with us there as, in their ignorance, many have thought He ought to have dealt with Esau and Jacob here—seeing only the good that was in Esau, and rewarding him for it with blessings he could not appreciate; and seeing only the evil in Jacob, not the good which blended with it, and punishing him not only according to his deserts, but above and beyond his deserts? If in this life on the whole I have tried to do God's will, and so pass for what is called " a good man," though I know only too well how much evil I have done, and how much evil still lurks in my nature which I am wholly unable to subdue, am I to be so rewarded for what God has made good in me as that no chastisement will be accorded me for that which has been evil, *i.e.*, no discipline by which I may be taught and enabled to subdue it? I should be sorry to think so: for how, except by such a discipline, am I ever to get quit of the evil that I hate? And if, on the whole, I have been a bad man; if, despite some pure affections and kindly deeds, I have been selfish in the main, and sensual, and godless, am I to be punished, as I deserve, for all that has been wrong in me, and yet to receive no recompense, no training, for that which has been good? Again, I should be sorry to think so: for that would neither be just nor kind. And if God is not going to deal both justly and kindly by me,—would God I had never been born! But if, because I have been a bad man, God will punish me as I know I deserve to be punished, if He will search me through and through with the discipline of his loving wrath till I hate all badness, and my own worst of all; if, because I have done a little good and have still some capacity of goodness in me, He will train and foster that capacity by the very discipline which also punishes me for my sins,—*that* will be both just and kind of Him, and my life is worth having after all. In that case I can say not simply, "The Lord is righteous," but, with the Psalmist,[1] "Thou, O Lord, art *merciful; for Thou renderest unto every man according to his work.*"

And whatever men may say, *that* is precisely what He will do, what He has bound Himself to do, by that solemn Law of Retribution which He has revealed

[1] Psalm lxii. 12.

in his Word. Was not St Paul a good man? and yet did not even he expect to appear before the judgment-seat of Christ, in order to receive the things done in his body, according to that he had done, whether it were good or bad?[1] Are we not expressly assured[2] that "*whatsoever* good thing *any man* doeth, the same shall he receive of the Lord?' And is not the term 'any man' wide enough to include even the worst of men? It is not easy to see how we could be more emphatically taught that the bad deeds of the good are to be weighed and condemned, and the good deeds of the bad to be weighed, approved, recompensed. Be sure, then, that you will find no injustice in the Great Judge of men. To *you* He will render according to your deeds, according to *all* your deeds, good as well as bad, bad as well as good; so that even the worst of you will not be quite shut out from hope, and even the best of you will receive the discipline and training which will tend to make you better, and still better, until you become perfect even as He is perfect. Else what becomes of the Law of Retribution which the Scriptures declare to rule in the world to come even as it rules in this? We see how that Law works here,—how variedly and subtlely, and with what delicate complexity it adjusts itself to the whole scale of our capacities, qualities, doings;

---

[1] 2 Corinthians v. 8-10.　　[2] Ephesians vi. 8.

and we may be sure that it will adapt itself with the same variety and subtlety to the whole of our nature and to all our deeds and qualities hereafter. In fine, God will prove Himself to be both " a *just* God, and a *Saviour.*"

Before I quit this point let me just remind you how exactly this conception of the Law of Retribution and its action in the world to come falls in with the laws formulated by modern science, and applied by it to the life and history of man ; viz., the laws of continuity and development. For as no man is wholly good and no man wholly bad ; and as, moreover, the man who is good on the whole is to receive according to his bad deeds as well as his good, and the man who is bad on the whole is to receive the due reward of his good deeds as well as of his bad, it follows that our life in the next æon, or age, will be as complex, as varied, as chequered as the present life : it follows that there will be no such sudden break in the continuity of our life as has often been assumed ; but that the next stage of it will be, as Science demands that it should be, the continuation and the development of that through which we are passing now : it follows, in short, that the life to come will be the present life carried to a higher power, with a larger scope and outlook, a nobler and severer discipline, a purer and a more enduring joy. On this point, at least,

Science and Scripture are at one and join in a pure concent.

There is another principle, or doctrine, which so pervades the whole structure of the Bible as to be even more familiar to us than the Law of Retribution. The *Unchangeableness of God* is as clearly revealed in Holy Writ as it is ingrained into the very reason of man. I need not quote a single text to prove it, nor allege a single argument. We all admit, we all believe it. But, though we believe that God sits high above all change, that He is the same yesterday, to-day, and for ever, we too often forget how this conviction should enter into and modify other theological beliefs which we hold to be equally true. If God is unchangeable, then what we see to be true of Him at any moment must be true of Him at every moment of time, true of Him also both before and after all the moments of time, always and for ever true of Him. But which of us remembers that, and allows for it, when he is trying to frame his doctrine of election, or to determine the true function of the punishments which dog the steps of sin, or to conceive the scope and method of that Atonement which taketh away the sin of the world ? " *The gifts, and the calling (i.e., the election) of God are without repentance,*" affirms St.

Paul;[1] *i.e.*, they are not to be revoked, not to be diverted from their purpose, not to be foiled and defeated of their end. But do we bear this affirmation sufficiently in mind when we are formulating our *credenda?* Let us briefly apply his conception of the Unchangeableness of God to the three doctrines I have just mentioned, and mark how it does or ought to modify them.

(2). Take, first, *the doctrine of Election.* As you recall what the Bible has to say on that point, you instantly remember that it consistently and throughout affirms that, when God calls or separates one man unto Himself, it is for the good of other men; that when He selects one family, it is that, in and through the one, all the families of the earth may be blessed: that when He chooses one nation, it is for the welfare of all nations,—"salvation," for example, being "*of* the Jews," but *for* the Gentiles as well as the Jews: that when He elects and establishes a church, it is for the spiritual benefit of the whole world. No man, no family, no nation, no church possesses any gift, any privilege, any superior capacity or power for its own use and welfare alone, but for the common advantage, the general good. You admit that to be the teaching of Scripture, as well as of Reason and Experience, do you not? But see where the admission

[1] Romans xi. 29.

lands you? The gifts and the election of the unchangeable God are as unchangeable as Himself, affirms St Paul; and, whatever we may do, *he* does not scruple to carry his principle to its full logical results. Thus, in those noble Chapters in his Epistle to the Romans, ix. to xi., he argues that, since God has called and chosen Israel, "*all* Israel must be saved," although, as he frankly admits, that stiffnecked race had long rejected the salvation of God. And if "all Israel" is to be saved, saved by the discipline of a coming age, since it certainly has not been saved in this age, who then can be lost? for who has sinned more deeply or with a more settled obstinacy? With the same logical consistency, the same impassioned earnestness, he argues, in Chapters v. and viii. of the same great Epistle, that as, by the unrighteousness of one, all men were condemned, so, by the righteousness of One, "*all* men" will be justified unto life; that the salvation of Christ will extend even beyond the limits of human sin: that even the inanimate creation, made subject to vanity and corruption by the sin of man, shall be redeemed from that involuntary bondage into the glorious liberty of the children of God. Clearly St Paul had "the courage of his convictions." It was plain to him that, sooner or later, the purposes of the unchanging God must be achieved in all their integrity and breadth. He was sure that Israel had been called in order that Israel might be saved, and that it might save the world; he was equally sure that by and through Christ *the world* had been called, and called in order that the whole human race might be saved: and therefore he was also sure that, by some means, in some of the ages, in the age to come if not in the present age, this redeeming purpose would be fulfilled, that both Israel and the world at large would be lifted into life everlasting. And even if we shrink from adopting this conclusion, if we believe that what the Apostle says in these Chapters must be limited by what he says elsewhere when his heart was not so hot and so large within him,[1] we may at least adopt his method of argument, and conclude:—What we see to be true of the unchanging God at any time must be true of Him through all the ages of time. Whenever, hitherto, He has elected a people for Himself, it has been that, through them, He might save and bless those who were less openly and avowedly favoured than they were. And, therefore, in the ages to come, if there be a saved and elect people, these too will be chosen not for their own sakes alone, and saved not

---

[1] This device of *limiting* Scripture by Scripture, which is a very different thing from "*comparing* Scripture with Scripture," and *striking an average of their contents*, is surely a very questionable one, and can hardly be resorted to by those who hold the stricter views of Inspiration without glaring and perilous inconsistency, though it is they who for the most part have recourse to it, especially when the scope of the larger and nobler Scriptures is to be curtailed.

simply that they may revel in their own blessedness, but that they may carry the tidings of salvation and the hope of blessedness to those who are still in the grasp of their sins.

But if that be so, how can the lot of those who even in that world are still tied and bound by the chain of their sins be a fixed and hopeless lot? God will not send us on a bootless errand, an errand in which success is impossible. If, then, this be the true doctrine of the Election, and we be of the elect, we may hope that in the ages to come God will make us the ambassadors of his love, and so bless us in our labour of love as that St Paul's largest hopes may be fulfilled, — "all Israel" and "the fulness of the Gentiles," *i.e.*, the whole race of man, being recovered to righteousness and life.

(3). We may draw a similar inference from *the true function of Punishment,* so soon as we see how the punitive—*i.e.*, the natural and inevitable—consequences of sin illustrate an invariable law of the kingdom and providence of the unchangeable God. Throughout the Bible we are taught that these miserable yet most happy consequences are designed by God to be corrective and even redemptive; that their true purpose is to castigate and chasten men, to open their eyes to the exceeding sinfulness of sin, to teach them to loathe and renounce it. What is the whole

Book of Job but a subtle and manifold commentary on this thesis,—that the sufferings of men are not simply penal and retributive, but corrective and remedial? that, by these, God is ever seeking to withdraw man from his evil deeds, to bring back his soul from the pit that it may grow light in the light of life? The Bible is full of statements and illustrations of this law of the Divine Kingdom—from which I select but two, one from the Old and one from the New Testament. The prophet Habakkuk, after that terrible description of the supreme judgment of his time with which his prophecy opens—viz., the invasion of " that fierce and impetuous nation," the Chaldeans, who " marched across the breadths of the earth, to seize upon dwelling-places not their own," whose aspect was cruel and fatal as the simoom and who " swept up captives like the sand,"—debated within himself what could be the meaning and purpose of this portentous "work" of God. And the conclusion to which he came was the simple conclusion of faith: Terrible and fatal as our doom seems, he argues " We shall not die;" for "*for judgment* hast Thou ordained it, O Lord, and Thou, O Rock, hast determined it *for correction*."[1] And this conclusion is still more simply and tenderly put in the Epistle to the Hebrews,[2] where we are exhorted neither to despise the chastening of the Lord, nor to

[1] Habakkuk i. 12.  [2] Hebrews xii. 5-11.

faint under it, since chastening is a mark of sonship: "for what son is he whom his father chasteneth not?" and because, though "no chastening for the present seemeth to be joyous, but grievous, nevertheless afterward it yieldeth *the peaceable fruit of righteousness unto them which are exercised thereby.*" ".Furthermore," argues the sacred Evangelist, expressly stating the law of all Divine chastisements, "we once had the fathers of our flesh to correct us, and we gave them reverence: shall we not much rather submit ourselves to the Father of spirits, and *live*. For they, verily, for a few days chastened us after their own liking; but He for our *profit, that we might be partakers of his holiness.*" Here, then, through this avenue, we get a glimpse into God's attitude toward the sins of men, of the purpose and function of the punishments with which He visits those sins. They are intended for correctio , for discipline, for our profit; they are designed to quicken life in us, to produce in us the peaceable fruits of righteousness, and even to make us partakers of the Divine holiness. But will the unchangeable God change his attitude toward sinful men, when, despite his discipline, they have gone down into the pit? Can He? If we have once seen what his purpose is in chastening and punishing them for their sins, must not that be his eternal, his unalterable, purpose? What right have we to assume that pain, and wrath, and judgment will have another function in the age to come, or in any age, than that which we know them to have in this age? If they are corrective and remedial here, why should they be penal and uncorrective hereafter, provided at least that the same God rules both here and there and rules by the same laws? They will not change their function and purpose. For has not Christ Himself taught us that even the unrighteous, who stand on his left hand on the very day of judgment, will go away from his presence into "an age-long *pruning*"? And what does that mean if not that the discipline of the world to come, like that of this world, is to be corrective and redemptive, to yield the peaceable fruit of righteousness? You do not prune a tree to kill it; but that it may bring forth fruit. And what but fruit, fruit unto holiness and life everlasting, can be the intention of the Divine pruning in the ages to come?

(4.) But, finally, the great doctrine, the doctrine which we need most of all to connect in our thoughts with the unchangeableness of God, is that of *the Atonement* wrought by Christ. We never weary of speaking of the Cross of Christ as a revelation of the loving and saving will of God, as a proof, and the supreme proof, of how far He will go, and how much He will do, to redeem men from their sins. But, O, what poor and unworthy conceptions of God do we entertain when we conceive of the great sacrifice of the Cross as a mere event in time, as an exception, though a most happy exception, to the ways of God, and not as a disclosure and an illustration of what He is always doing for men! We are so bound by the measures of time within which we live, that we even *think* within them, and find it well nigh impossible to conceive of an eternal law, an eternal action, an eternal passion. Although the Scriptures often speak of the sacrifice of Christ as both ordained and made *from before the foundation of the world*, and thus seek to lift it clean out of the limits of time, we commonly think of it only as a sacrifice made on a certain sacred day in our human calendar. And yet the Cross of Christ must speak to us of an eternal sacrifice, it must become the symbol of a divine and eternal passion, before we can rise to an adequate conception of its significance. In what sense, then, is Christ "the Lamb slain from before the foundation of the world?" in what sense is the Cross an exponent, an illustration, of the eternal passion of God?

That I may not even unconsciously invent or modify a theory that shall sustain my argument, permit me to answer that question in words which I printed twelve years ago,[1] when I was thinking only

---

[1] The passage is a condensed citation from a discourse on the Self-Sacrifice taught by the Sacrifice of Christ, published in a small volume called "The Secret of Life," which has long been out of print.

of the Atonement wrought by Christ, and not of the future conditions of men. "God made men, as He was obliged to do, if they were not to be mere automata moved by a Divine spring, free to choose between good and evil. And, though good be in itself so winsome and attractive, men chose evil rather than good. In proving and asserting the freedom of their will, they deflected it from the will of God. It was, and is, the Divine purpose to redeem them, through their experience of the miseries of self-will backed by the ministries of his grace, to a firm and constant love of goodness, to draw back their wills into a complete and abiding harmony with his perfect Will. *This* is the one, divine, far-off event to which the whole Creation moves, and the whole course of Providence, and the entire series of Revelations, and all the gifts and operations of the Spirit. To secure this result, God permits those who have made an evil choice to *do* the evil they have chosen, and to suffer by and for it, to be corrected by it. But God is love, and cannot see his creatures suffer without pain. God is good, and cannot come into contact with evil, even though it be a victorious contact, without entering into a divine agony. In all our afflictions *He* is afflicted; He suffers in all our sufferings. That is to say, from the very beginning God has borne part, and the greater part, in the countless and dreadful miseries and conflicts which men have provoked by their sins, and will continue to bear that part in them till sin and time shall be no more.

"Now it is this perpetual conflict with the innumerable forms of evil, this endurance of the miseries which his creatures endure, this sorrow as of a gracious Father who sees his children sold into the bitter captivity of sin and pain, and can only suffer with them till, through suffering, they have grown wiser and stronger,—it is *this* which constitutes the eternal agony and passion of God; this is the cross which He for ever bears, this the sacrifice which He is always making for the sin of the world.

"But if this divine eternal Passion is to become a redeeming energy, it must be revealed to those for whom it is endured. Till we *know* that God is sorry for us, we shall not be sorry for ourselves with that godly sorrow which worketh life. Till we *feel* that He is afflicted in all our afflictions, and will therefore use all the resources of his power to deliver us from the evils which afflict us, we can make no hopeful stand against them. Hence, once in the ages, in the person of Jesus Christ, God became man to shew his sympathy with men, his kinship with them, his care for them. To prove that He is verily afflicted in our afflictions, and that He is able to redeem us out of them all, He visibly lived our life, bare our afflictions, carried our sorrows, confronted our temptations, and overcame even the sharpness of death by laying down his life for us and by taking it again. In short, the historical Cross of Christ is simply a disclosure within the bounds of time and space of the eternal passion of the unchangeable God; it is simply the supreme manifestation of that redeeming Love which always suffers in our sufferings, and is for ever at work for our salvation from them."

For, as we have seen, what is in the eternal unchanging God at any moment must always be in Him. Christ did not create, He only unveiled and disclosed, the self-sacrificing love of the Father. His attitude toward man and the evil that is in man, if at any instant we can catch a glimpse of it, must be his constant unvarying attitude, since He is the same yesterday, to-day, and for ever. In Christ and his cross we get not a glimpse only, but a full view of his attitude toward us and toward the evil that is in us: and *that* must be his constant attitude. As once, so always, He suffers in our sufferings; as once, so always, He is seeking to save us from the evil which causes them: or how can He be unchangeably the same? In every age, in every world, *that* must be his work, his endeavour for us: for what is there in the mere lapse of time, or change of place, to affect Him who sits high above change and time? If God suffers with me here, because I am his creature, his child, must He not suffer with me hereafter, when my sufferings may be so much more keen and deep? If He here seeks to redeem me, and has even endured the bitter Cross to encourage me to believe and hope in his redeeming love, can He, all in a moment, cease to care for my redemption and to labour for it, and study why and how He may degrade and torment me? It is incredible, impossible. Changeable and fickle as men are, would any man that is a father do that? And God is unchangeable. His gifts and election are without repentance. The mere lapse of time, the fact that I have passed out of this age into the age to come, cannot change Him, cannot annul his relation to me, his sympathy with me, cannot reverse his whole attitude toward me.

> " Love is not love that alters where it alteration finds,
> Or bends with the remover to remove."

And if human love can resist the influences of time and change, shall not the eternal love of God?

You see, then, how many great doctrines, how many leading and pervading principles of the Bible, combine to assure us that we have misinterpreted those passages which speak of the future condition of the impenitent, if at least we have taken them to imply that all who are not saved in this age will be doomed, the very instant they die, to an endless and depraving torment. Such an interpretation is inconsistent with the law of Retribution, with the doctrine of Election, with the revealed function of Punishment, and even with the very love and passion of God as disclosed in the Atonement wrought by Christ.

## VIII.—UNIVERSAL REDEMPTION.

I MAY now assume, I think, that the main conclusions at which we have arrived are tolerably familiar to you, or that they may be recalled to your memories by a mere touch.

We have seen, then, that the English verb "to damn" is used to translate two Greek words which never mean more than "to condemn," and commonly mean only "to judge;" that our English noun "hell" is employed to render three Greek substantives—Tartarus, Hades, Gehenna, each of which, so far from indicating an endless state of torment, indicates only an intermediate and temporary condition of the soul; that the Greek and English adjective "æonial," though it is commonly translated by "eternal" or "everlasting," means only æon- or age- long both in the Bible and out of it; and we have found, especially in the writings of St Paul, a Christian doctrine of the æons, a doctrine which implies that as there have been ages that are past during which men have been slowly raised to their present condition, so also there are ages to come in which the Divine education and development of the race will be carried on toward its final issue or goal. From all these lines of thought, and from the Scriptures which illustrate them, we have drawn the conclusion that the impenitent wicked, when they pass out of this age, will not be adjudged to a final and changeless doom, but will be exposed to a still severer and more searching discipline than that of this life,—to what our Lord Himself calls an " æonial pruning," or a " salting with fire," the design of which will be to free them from their thraldom to evil, and to save them unto life everlasting. The current theory of the future estate of the wicked is, therefore, condemned by the very Scriptures to which it has long made its appeal.

Nor only so. It is also at variance, not only with the general tone and spirit of the revelation made by Christ—though that were much, but also with certain definite principles, or doctrines, which are wrought into the very substance of Scripture and pervade it from end to end. It is inconsistent with the law of Retribution, with the doctrine of Election, with the declared function and end of Punishment, and with the eternal love and passion of God as disclosed in the Atonement wrought by our Lord Jesus Christ.

At this point we arrived, and paused, in our last Lecture. And, having conducted the argument so far, it might seem that nothing remained but to review its whole course, and to formulate some reasonable and coherent theory of the life to come. But even yet the argument is not complete; and the endeavour to frame a theory must still be postponed, if indeed we should ever brace ourselves to enter on a path of speculation so lofty and so perilous. For the present I must be content with carrying the argument to a close, by adducing those Scriptures which either expressly affirm or obviously imply *the universality of the redemption* wrought by God in and through Christ Jesus our Lord. And, unless you have made a special study of this subject for yourselves, I cannot doubt that you will be astonished, I trust also that your best hopes for mankind will be invigorated and confirmed, by finding how numerous and emphatic these Scriptures are, how the principle they illustrate is interwoven with the very texture, and with the whole texture, of Holy Writ.

From the dawn of Revelation down to its latest recorded utterance we find the very widest scope assigned to the redeeming purpose and work of God our Saviour. Even in those early days when one man, one family, one nation were successively chosen to be the depositories of Divine Truth; when, therefore, if ever we might expect to find the redemptive purpose of God disclosed within narrow and local limitations, when unquestionably it was in much fettered and restrained by personal promises and by national and temporary institutions, that Divine purpose is for ever overleaping every limit, every transient localization and restraint, and claiming as its proper sphere "all the souls that are" and shall be. Thus, for example, Abraham and his family are chosen for special teaching and privilege; but it is in order that in him and them "*all the families of the earth,*" without distinction of name and race, and whatever the moral condition to which they have sunk, "may be blessed."[1]

In what sense this great promise was meant, how wide and far-reaching its scope, we are taught by two of the greatest Christian apostles. St Peter standing in the temple at Jerusalem, and addressing part of that vast multitude "out of every nation under heaven" which had come together to keep the sacred Feasts that immediately followed the death of Christ,—many of whom, remember, had clamoured for his death and invoked his blood on their heads—did not scruple to say to them,[2] "*Ye* are the children of the covenant which God made with our fathers, saying unto Abraham, And in thy seed shall *all the kindreds of the earth* be blessed. Unto you *first* God, having raised up his son Jesus, sent Him to bless you, in turning away *every one of you* from his iniquities." This, then, as St Peter read it, was the blessing promised to Abraham and his family,—the blessing of

[1] Genesis xii. 3; and xxii. 18.   Acts iii. 25, 26.

becoming a blessing. They themselves were to be redeemed from iniquity, to be recovered to righteousness, by Him who was at once the seed of Abraham and the Son of God; but they were to be saved in order that from and through them this great salvation might extend to "*every one*" of the Jews and to "*all the kindreds*" of the earth. This salvation had indeed been sent to the Jews "first;" but that very word "first" implied that it was to be sent to the Gentiles also.

And what St Peter both implies and asserts St Paul emphatically confirms. Writing to the Celtic and Asiatic tribes of Galatia, he argues [1] that as many as believe in Christ become, by their very faith, children of faithful Abraham; and affirms: "The Scripture, *foreseeing that God would justify the heathen* through faith, preached beforehand the Gospel unto Abraham, saying, In thee shall *all nations* be blessed."

Both the holy Apostles therefore saw, and teach us to see, in the promise made to Abraham a disclosure of the Divine intention to redeem men, to make them just, or righteous, by the Gospel of his Son; and both affirm that this intention extends to the whole family of man, though the one applies it mainly to the Jewish tribes and the other to the

[1] Galatians iii. 8.

nations of the Gentiles. St Peter, indeed, does not shrink even from asserting that this blessing has been "*sent*," has been conferred upon the most flagrant and enormous sinners the world then held,—those who, because they loved darkness rather than light, had with lawless hands put to death the very Life of men.

And from the time at which this great and far-reaching promise, or gospel, was given to Abraham, the universal scope of the Divine Redemption is insisted on with growing emphasis even in those Hebrew Scriptures which we too often assume to be animated only by a local and national spirit. That such a spirit is to be found in them is unquestionable; but it is equally unquestionable that from the very first we may also find in them a generous and catholic spirit which contemplates the salvation of the whole world, and that this deeper broader spirit more and more disengages itself from all that is national and local in them as the years roll on. The Psalmists, for example, are full of the happiest and largest forecasts. When they speak of the coming Messiah they are at the furthest remove from claiming the blessings of his reign exclusively for themselves. On the contrary they say, "His name shall endure for ever; his name shall be continued as long as the sun: and *men* shall be blessed in Him; *all nations* shall call Him blessed."[1]

[1] Psalm lxxii. 17.

They look forward to an age when "*the heathen* shall fear the name of the Lord, and *the kingdoms* shall serve Him."[1] They constantly breathe forth the invitation, "O praise the Lord *all ye nations*; praise Him *all ye peoples*,[2]—an invitation, by the bye, which St Paul cites when he is arguing that Jesus Christ was sent, not only to confirm and fulfil the promises made to the Hebrew fathers, but also "that *the Gentiles* might glorify God for his mercy."[3] And, in fine, the Psalter closes with the noble, far-resounding, yet most characteristic, strain, "*Let everything that hath breath* praise the Lord."[4]

Nor do the Prophets come behind the Psalmists of Israel; rather they excel them in the large gladness with which they recognize the breadth and length, the height and depth of the Divine Redemption. I need not detain you by quoting the noble strains in which Isaiah and the major prophets depict the golden close of time, the age, or ages, during which a regenerated race is to dwell on a renovated earth. They are familiar to you; they have entered into the heart and reappeared in the poetry of all Christian races. From him who, because he so clearly foresaw the day of Christ, has been christened "the Evangelical Prophet" take only this one sentence; and take it mainly

[1] Psalm cii. 15, 22.  [2] Psalm cxvii. 1.
[3] Romans xv. 11.  [4] Psalm cl. 6.

because St Paul echoes it back, and interprets it as he echoes it. It is Jehovah who speaks these words by the mouth of Isaiah: " Look unto me, and be ye saved, *all ye ends of the earth*; for I am God, and there is none other: I have sworn by myself, the word is gone out of my mouth in righteousness and shall not return, That unto me *every knee shall bend, and every tongue shall vow.*"[1] Could any words more emphatically declare it to be the Divine purpose that the whole earth, to the very ends of it, shall be saved, that every knee shall bow in homage before God and every tongue take the oath of fealty to Him? Are we not expressly told that this declaration, since it has come from the righteous mouth of God, cannot return to Him void, but must accomplish its object,—that object being the salvation of the human race? St Paul echoes this great word, and interprets it in his Epistle to the Philippians;[2] and though on his lips it gains definiteness and precision, assuredly it loses no jot nor tittle of its breadth. He affirms that, because Christ did not clutch at his equality with the Father, but, to fulfil God's ancient promise, humbled Himself to manhood, to servitude, to death, therefore " God hath highly exalted Him, and given Him a name which is above every name, in order that at the Name of Jesus *every knee should bow*"—not only every knee of man,

[1] Isaiah xlv. 22, 23.     [2] Philippians ii. 6-11.

for now the promise grows incalculably wider, but every knee—"*in heaven, and in earth, and under the earth;* and that *every tongue* should confess that Jesus Christ is Lord, to the glory of God the Father." It is hard to understand Isaiah as proclaiming less than an universal redemption; but if St Paul did not mean to proclaim a redemption as wide as the universe, what use or force is there in words?

I have said enough, however, to recall to your memories the bright and vivid pictures of "the Regeneration" which the greater prophets—such as Isaiah, Ezekiel, Daniel—loved to paint. If you would collect them in some private gallery of your own, you know where to look for them. But, perhaps, some of you may not be equally familiar with the fact that these same pictures, drawn on a proportionally lesser scale, are also to be found in the works of those whom we call the Minor Prophets—giving them that name not because their strains are of an inferior quality to those of their compeers, but because they are fewer and shorter. Yet every one of their brief poems, or collections of poems, has its tiny apocalypse. And—mark this point well, for it will be useful to us by and bye—while each of the Minor Prophets sees the vision of a whole world redeemed to the love and service of righteousness, this vision of redemption is invariably accompanied by a vision of judgment. Thus, for instance, Joel[1] foresees that all nations will be gathered into the Valley of Doom in order that every man may receive the due reward of his deeds; but he also foresees that they will be judged in order that, thereafter, the Spirit of God may be poured out on "*all flesh,*" on young men and maidens, old men and children, bond and free. In like manner the pencil of Habakkuk[2] labours to depict the judgment that will fall on the nations which "exhaust themselves for vanity;" but he too can look beyond the terrors of judgment and see "*the whole earth* filled with the knowledge of the glory of God as the waters cover the deep." Zephaniah,[3] again, is possessed by this deep conviction, this healing and sustaining hope. He sees that God will make Himself terrible over the nations only that "*all the isles of the heathen, every one from its place,* may worship Him;" that He will purify the earth with the fire of his judgments, in order that He may "turn *to the nations* a pure lip," in order that they may "*all* invoke the name of Jehovah, and serve Him with one shoulder." And Malachi,[4] the last of the prophets, foresees a day of the Lord, which will burn like a furnace against all unrighteousness of men; but he also foresees that these flaming judgments will kindle on men only that "*from the rising of the sun*

---

[1] Joel ii. 28-31; and iii. 12-21.   [2] Habakkuk ii. 13, 14.
[3] Zephaniah ii. 11; and iii. 8, 9.   [4] Malachi i. 11; iii. 1-3; iv. 1-.3

*to the going down thereof* God's name may be great *among the nations*," and that "*in every place* incense may be burned to his Name and a pure sacrifice be offered Him."

But why should I elaborate this point? why should I cite so many passages from the Old Testament Scriptures, except indeed to impress upon you the fact that even in those Scriptures which we admit to be the narrowest in their scope this doctrine of an universal redemption is iterated and reiterated again and again? We, who are appealing to the authority of Holy Writ, need no proof of the fact, though we may need to have the fact impressed upon us: for St Peter,[1] when he is speaking of "*the times of the restitution of all things*," *i.e.*, the age in which all things shall be restored to their primeval, or raised to their ideal, order and beauty, distinctly asserts that God hath spoken of this age " by the mouth of *all his holy prophets since the world began*."

Here, then, we have the highest and most conclusive authority for believing that, from the beginning, God has cherished the purpose of an universal restoration or redemption; that this purpose has been revealed to and by all the inspired Hebrew prophets: and that the revelation made to them has been endorsed and attested by the Christian Apostles. It would almost

[1] Acts iii. 21.

seem unnecessary, therefore, that I should go on to quote the illustrations of this Divine purpose which abound in the Scriptures of the New Testament. But the effect of a doctrine depends not only on the clearness and fullness with which it is revealed, but also on the clearness and depth of the impression it makes on our minds. And hence I will cite, as briefly and with as little comment as I can, some of the leading passages of the New Testament in which this great doctrine is taught or implied.

John the Baptist, then, saw in Jesus "the Lamb of God which taketh away (not the sins, but) *the sin of the world;*" *i.e.*, the whole sin of the whole world.[1] The Lord Jesus Himself assures us that "God sent his Son into the world not to condemn the world, but *that the world through him might be saved.*"[2] And, again, "The Father loveth the Son, and hath given *all things* into his hand," and "*all that the Father hath given me shall come to me,* and him that cometh to me I will in no wise cast out;" for I came down from heaven, not to do mine own will, but the will of Him that sent me: and *this is the Father's will who hath sent me, that of all which He hath given me I should lose nothing, but should raise it up again at the last day.*"[3] And, again, "*I*, if I be lifted up from

---

[1] St John i. 29.      [2] *Ibid.*, iii. 17.
[3] *Ibid.*, iii. 35; and vi. 37-39.

the earth, *will draw all men unto me.*"[1] Could even He that formed the tongue use language more explicit and decisive than this? Could even the Lord Jesus have taught us more plainly—and more effectively if only we bring an unbiassed mind to his words—that it is the intention and purpose of God to take away the sin of the whole race, and to redeem all men unto Himself? And since the gifts and the calling of God are without repentance, must not that purpose be carried out, if not in this age, then in some of the ages to come?

But lest we should have misunderstood these great sayings of the Great Teacher, let us mark how the Apostles understood them, what meanings they found in them. The great theologians of the Apostolic Company were St Paul and St John. St John has left us only one theological Epistle, only one public Letter, from which we may learn how the truths taught by Christ shaped themselves in his mind and ministry. But even in this single and brief Letter we find these sayings and such as these: "And we have seen and do testify that the Father sent the Son to be *the Saviour of the world;*"[2] and, again, "If any man sin, we have an Advocate with the Father, Jesus Christ the Righteous; and He is the propitiation for our sins, *and not for ours only, but also for those of the world.*"[3]

[1] St John xii. 32.   [2] 1 John iv. 14.   [3] *Ibid.*, ii. 1, 2.

St Paul, happily, has left us many Epistles; and in *his* Letters the doctrine of universal redemption is developed at length and with extraordinary breadth and force. Writing to the Ephesians[1] on that "mystery" of the Divine Will with which we are now concerned, the redemption of the human race, he calls it "God's good pleasure which He hath purposed in Christ," and affirms this purpose to be "that in the dispensation of the fulness of times He might gather up under one head in Christ *all things, both which are in heaven and which are on earth,* even in Him in whom also we have obtained an inheritance." That is to say, it is God's good purpose, in and by the Christian economy, to gather up "*the all*"—the whole universe of intelligent creatures, whether in heaven or on earth—under the lordship and rule of Christ. Not only are those who then believed and who by faith had obtained an inheritance in Christ, included in this purpose, but all spirits in heaven and on earth; and not these spirits alone, but also the very universe in which they dwell: for only thus do we exhaust the meaning of that "all" (τὰ πάντα) which is to be reduced to the love and obedience of Christ. Writing to the Colossians,[2] he expresses the same thought in other words; for to them he declares it to be the pleasure of the Father that all the fulness of the Divine Nature

---

[1] Ephesians i. 10.      [2] Colossians i. 20.

should dwell in Christ, in order that, "having made peace through the blood of the Cross, *He might reconcile all things* (τὰ πάντα) *unto Himself,* whether they be things on earth or things in heaven:" the two points on which the Apostle here lays stress being (1) the universality of the reconciliation to be effected by Christ, and (2) the fact that Christ is the only medium of that reconciliation.

Writing to the Romans,[1] he presents us with another aspect of this doctrine, and reaches the same conclusion by another road, the road of the Hebrew prophets. He is rebuking the disciples at Rome for judging one another for mere differences of thought and practice. Judgment belongs to the Lord, he argues, and to Him alone, whether in this life or in that which is to come; for "whether we live, we live unto the Lord; and whether we die, we die unto the Lord; whether we live, therefore, or die, we are the Lord's." And then he adds this remarkable passage: "For *to this end* Christ both died, and rose and revived, *that He might be Lord both of the dead and of the living.* But why dost thou judge thy brother? . . . for we shall all stand before the judgment-seat of Christ. For it is written, As I live, saith the Lord, *every knee* shall bow to me, and *every tongue* shall confess to God." Christ is to be the Lord, then, of

[1] Romans xiv. 9-11.

the dead as well as of the living; and, as "no man can confess that Jesus is the Lord but by the Holy Ghost," the dead who are to bow to Him and confess Him their Lord, as well as the living, must be open to the renewing ministry of the Divine Spirit: open to it! yes, and mercifully condemned and exposed to it until "every one," even the most stubborn, be compelled to yield it. Here, too, strangely enough, and in this St Paul resembles the Hebrew prophets,[1] there is obviously some connection in his thoughts between *the judgment* to which both the living and the dead are to be summoned, and their participation in the life and Kingdom of Christ.

Again; what less than a purpose of universal redemption can explain such passages as these: "God was in Christ, *reconciling the world unto Himself, not imputing their trespasses unto them:*"[2] "We trust in the living God, who is *the Saviour of all men, specially of those who believe:*"[3] "I exhort, therefore, that supplications, prayers, intercessions, thanksgivings be made *for all men:* for this is good and acceptable in the sight of God our Saviour, *who wills that all men should be saved, and should come to a full recognition of the truth,* since there is one Mediator between God and men, the Man Christ Jesus, who gave Himself a ransom *for all* (ὑπὲρ πάντων),—a fact to be

[1] See page 180 *et seq.*   [2] 2 Corinthians v. 19.   [3] 1 Timothy iv. 10.

testified in its appropriate seasons."[1] Now surely these passages speak for themselves, and need no interpreter, at least to those who have "the mind of Christ," and instinctively reject whatever is contrary to the great revelation He came to make. On any narrower hypothesis than ours they must be pared down, explained away, their generous force abated; but on the hypothesis which we have, at least provisionally, formed, they are simple and clear as day and may be taken, as surely Divine Words should be taken, in their largest sense. On that hypothesis we read them thus. The whole world of men is ultimately to be redeemed to the love and service of Righteousness by God our Saviour, and so to be really and eternally *reconciled* to Him. But if He is to be ultimately the Saviour of *all* men, as it is very certain that a countless multitude of men are not saved in this age, they must of necessity be excluded from that presence and glory of the Lord in the age to come which the righteous will enjoy, must be exposed to a far more severe and searching discipline than any they have known here, in order that what the discipline of this age has failed to do may be done—*i.e.*, that they may be redeemed from the hand of their iniquities and led, through righteousness, unto life eternal. God therefore, while the Saviour of all men, is specially the

[1] 1 Timothy ii. 1, 3, 6.

Saviour of them that believe, since these are saved in the present age, will pass into the blessedness of a perfecting discipline in the age to come, and may even be employed on errands of mercy to the spirits who are still in the bonds of their iniquity. Meanwhile, the purpose of God standeth sure. It is his will, his good pleasure, that all men should be saved by being led, through whatever correction and training may be necessary for that end, to a full and hearty recognition of the truth ; which truth will be testified to them in its appropriate seasons, and by appropriate methods, in the ages to come, if it has not been brought home to them here : so appropriately and so forcibly testified that at last they will no longer be able to withstand it, but will heartily betake themselves to the Father against whom they have sinned, and submit themselves to his righteous Will through the Mediator, the Man Christ Jesus. *Thus*, as I read St Paul, God will prove Himself to be at once the Saviour of all men, and especially the Saviour of those who now turn to Him.

And that I am not forcing a meaning on his words alien to his mind is proved by those other passages from his writings which I have already quoted. It is still more conclusively proved by the two great passages in his Epistle to the Romans in which he formally argues for the salvation of the whole Hebrew race and for that of the world at large. We referred to these passages only in the previous Lecture ; and therefore I need now do no more than remind you that, in Chapters ix. to xi. of this Epistle, the Apostle proves, at least to his own satisfaction and comfort, both that "*all Israel* will be saved," and that "*the fulness of the Gentiles*" will be brought in to the kingdom of God ; in short, that "God hath concluded all men in unbelief," or "shut up all in sin," only "*that He may have mercy on all* :" while in Chapters v. and viii. he argues at great length that "as in Adam all die, so in Christ shall *all* be made alive,"[1] that as sin has abounded, so the grace of God shall much more abound, that the free gift of that grace shall come on "*all*" men "*unto justification of life* ;" and that even the inanimate creation, reduced to the bondage of vanity and corruption through the sin of man, shall be redeemed into the glorious liberty of the sons of God. In his first Epistle to the Corinthians [2] he iterates and completes this argument ; not only affirming that *all* shall be made alive by Christ, but affirming also that Christ must reign until He has brought all who have ranked themselves among his enemies to his feet : that "the end" of the Christian

---

[1] These words are from 1 Corinthians xv. 22, where we have both a confirmation and a briefer statement of his argument in the Romans.

[2] 1 Corinthians xv. 24-28.

dispensation cannot come until all *are* subdued under Him ; and that then even He Himself will become " subject " unto the Father—in the same sense surely in which his enemies have been subjected to Him, *i.e.,* voluntarily, gladly, of freewill, not of constraint—in order that God may be all, not in, some only, nor only in many, but *in all.*

Now is it not well nigh impossible to gather these passages together from the Old Testament and the New, to listen to this " pure concent " of the Hebrew Prophets and the Christian Apostles with the direct words of Jehovah and of Christ, without being convinced that the doctrine of an universal redemption and restitution, however long we may have overlooked it, is interwoven with the very texture of Holy Writ and pervades it from end to end ? And how is the eternal purpose of the unchangeable God to be accomplished if there be no possibilities of salvation beyond the grave, when it is only too certain that many pass out of this life loving darkness rather than light, many more to whom the good news of Redemption have never been either adequately or attractively presented, and most of all who have never so much as heard the joyful sound ?

I am not unmindful of the fact that he who so searches the Scriptures as to find this happy prospect of eternal life for all men in them, will also find many passages which denounce the wrath of God against all unrighteousness of men, which threaten the wicked with the terrors of judgment, with death, and with being destroyed from the presence of the Lord and the glory of his power. We have examined many of these passages, and have ascertained what they mean. It is no part of our argument that wrath and judgment and punishment are not to be elements of the life to come. Rather we affirm, and rejoice to affirm, that in every age and in every world unrighteousness must be hateful to God; and that so long as men cleave to it, and refuse to submit themselves to the righteousness of God, they must be searched through and through with unspeakable miseries. We admit that if men pass out of this age unrighteous and impenitent, they must be banished from the presence and glory of God in the age to come, must pass through the pangs of death before they can be born again into life. But we ask why death, judgment, punishment should change their nature and function the very moment we pass from this æon, or life, into the next? They are remedial and corrective here; why should they be uncorrective and merely punitive hereafter? On the authority of the New Testament itself we maintain that God is the Father of the spirits of all flesh, and that He can never chasten us save for our profit. Nay, more, on the authority both of the Hebrew Prophets and of the Christian Apostles we maintain that this law of the Divine punishments holds in the world to come no less than in the present world, since their visions of future judgment are almost invariably followed by visions of a redemption which is to extend to all nations and to cover the whole earth. And this conclusion is sustained by our Lord Himself in those memorable passages in which He speaks of the unrighteous as going away from his bar into "an agelong pruning," and affirms that "every one shall be *salted* with fire," *i.e.*, saved by it.

Still there are those who are well nigh incapable of logic, well nigh impervious to argument, even when the argument is based on Scripture itself, who distrust inferences and demand instances. And these may say: "Before we accept this doctrine of an universal redemption to be achieved in due time, before we even weigh your argument for it, can you point us to any instance of the redemption of sinful men after they had left this life, after they had been condemned to receive the due reward of their deeds?" And even to that question, unreasonable though it be, I may reply, "Yes, I can." In the first Epistle of St Peter (Chapter iii. verses 18-20) we are distinctly told that, when Jesus was put to death in the flesh, He descended in the spirit to that dim Hadean world in which, as the Jews held, the spirits of all men await the Resurrection, and preached his Gospel "*to the spirits in prison,*" to those who were being held in ward until the trumpet should sound and the dead be raised up. Nor was it to the spirits of the righteous alone that He preached this Gospel, but also to those who had been "disobedient" to the word of God, to that ungodly generation to which Noah had preached righteousness in vain,—a generation so disobedient and ungodly that it repented God He had made them, and compelled Him to sweep them off the face of the earth with a flood. Do you ask, "For what purpose, and to what effect, did He preach to them?" St Peter replies in the same Epistle (Chap. iv. ver. 6): "For *this* cause was the Gospel preached also *to them that are dead, that they might* be judged according to men in the flesh, but *live according to God in the spirit.*" Now we know how this strange revelation made to St Peter was interpreted by the primitive Church—and this is a point which those should mark who object to the late and modern date of the doctrine of Universal Redemption; for within a hundred years of the death of St John there appeared a work of fiction, called the Gospel of Nicodemus, which professed to set forth all the details of Christ's descent into Hades. Of course this Fiction speaks to us with an authority no greater than that of the "Pilgrim's Progress," although, when it appeared, it was very widely received as an authoritative description of our Lord's ministry in Hades. But just as from Bunyan's great Allegory we might very safely infer what the Puritan conception of the Christian life was in the seventeenth century, so from this "Gospel of Nicodemus" we may very safely infer what conceptions the Christians of the second century formed of Christ's descent into Hades. And in this Gospel it is expressly affirmed,[1] that, when He arrived, the gates of the Hadean prison burst open before Him, and the King of Glory, taking our forefather Adam by the hand, and turning to the vast multitude of imprisoned spirits, said, "*Come all with me, as many as have died through the tree which he touched;* for, behold, I raise you all up through the tree of the Cross,"—words which, after all, are but a paraphrase of St Paul's great saying, "As by one man's disobedience the many were made sinners, so by the obedience of One shall the many be made righteous."

This, then, was the faith of the early Church, before it became corrupted by heathen philosophies and heathen superstitions—viz., that the good news brought to earth by Christ was also preached by Him in Hades, preached even in Gehenna; that on the bridge of his Cross even the worst of the spirits in torment were able to pass over the "great gulf" and enter into the

[1] The Gospel of Nicodemus, Part II., Chap. 8.

joys of Paradise ; that even the disobedient generation of Noah, though still " dead " in the judgment and censures of men, live unto God. Why should it not be our faith too ? St Paul held it as well as St Peter ; for in all those passages [1] in which he speaks of the redemption of Christ as extending to all who are in heaven, and on the earth, and *under the earth,* by those who are "*under* the earth," he signified the inhabitants of that vast subterranean kingdom in which, as he held, the spirits of the dead were reserved for the day of judgment. And St John held it as well as St Paul; for, in his Apocalyptic vision,[2] he too beheld " *every creature* in heaven, and on the earth, and *under the earth,*"—*i.e.,* in Hades, giving glory and power unto Him that sitteth on the throne, and unto the Lamb for ever and ever.

And if St Peter held the faith that even the most disobedient of the spirits in prison were quickened into life by the preaching of Christ ; if St Paul held that every knee in the Hadean kingdom should bow to Christ, as well as every knee in heaven and on earth, and every tongue confess Him Lord, which yet no man can do but by the Holy Ghost: if St John heard " every creature " in hades as well as in heaven and on earth, singing the high praises of God and the Lamb,—why should not we also hold this faith ? If

[1] Cf. Philippians ii. 9-11.     [2] Rev. v. 13.

Christ took flesh and dwelt among us that He might become at all points like as we are and throw open the kingdom of heaven to all believers; if He trod, step by step, the path we have to travel from the cradle to the grave,—must He not also, for us men and our salvation, have passed on into that dim unknown region on which our spirits enter when we die? Did He leave, did He forsake our path at the very moment when it sinks into a darkness we cannot penetrate, just when, to us at least, it seems to grow most lonely, most critical, most perilous? And if He followed our path to the end, and passed into that awful and mysterious world into which we also must soon pass, could his Presence be hid? Must not truth and mercy, righteousness and love attend Him wherever He goes? Would not the eternal Gospel in his heart find fit and effectual utterance, and the very darkness of Hades be illuminated and dispersed as it was traversed by the Light of Life? Surely our own reason confirms the revelations of Scripture, and constrains us to believe that, in all worlds and in all ages, as in this, Christ will prove Himself to be the great Lord and Lover of men, and will claim all souls for his own.

## IX.—WHAT WE SHALL BE.

WHEN we were commencing our study, at the very outset of these Lectures, I forewarned you that, in all probability, we should find in the Word of God no clear and detailed disclosures of the final estate whether of the good or of the bad; and that for this reason. Just as it is impossible to convey to a child many of the facts, relations, and intercourses of mature human life, *i.e.*, of its own subsequent career, so, probably, it is impossible that the higher facts of the life which is purely spiritual and eternal, *i.e.*, the ultimate facts and conditions of our own career, should be conveyed to us at this early and initial stage of it, and while we are under the conditions of sense and time. If St Paul, when he was rapt in the spirit into Paradise, beheld scenes which he could not depict and heard what he calls "unwordable words," words, *i.e.*, which could not be uttered, much more, had he been caught up into the very heaven of heavens, would he have found himself surrounded by sacred and august realities which it is not possible for man to conceive, much less describe. My warning has been abundantly verified. Although we have now studied most of the leading passages in the Gospels and Epistles which relate to the future life of the human race, we have found none as yet which carries us beyond the æons of time. While the New Testament has much to tell us of our future conditions, it has nothing, or nothing definite, to say of our final estate, but compels us, in so far as that is concerned, to "*trust* in the living God who is the Saviour of all men," and in a very special sense the Saviour of all who believe in Him. And, indeed, there hardly can be a *final* estate for finite creatures such as we are. We must ever be reaching forth to things before and beyond us, ever rising through grade after grade of being and of attainment, ever approaching yet never reaching that infinite perfection which we name God.

For the present, at all events, we must be content with the revelation which He has made of "the ages to come," the ages which are to succeed this present age and to precede that great "day of judgment" beyond which as yet we cannot, for want of clearer light, safely project our thoughts.

Now as we try to sum up all that we have learned of those future but intermediate ages, there rises before us the image of a vast Hadean world, with its Paradise for the good and its Gehenna for the bad, in which the spirits of all who have left this life are assembled, in order that every man may receive according to his deeds, but receive also according to the infinite mercy and goodness of God.  And if we try to conceive the moral and spiritual conditions of this Hadean world, we derive no little help from the fact that in the Scriptures of the New Testament God is described as "the æonial God," the Holy Spirit as "the æonial Spirit," and the redemption of Christ as an "æonial redemption," *i.e.* a redemption which it will take many æons, or ages, to complete.  For these descriptions assure us that our God and Father will rule over all the ages to come as well as over this present age; that through all these ages the Holy Spirit, our Comforter, will still be at work in the hearts of men, seeking to change them into the image and likeness of God : and that the redemption of Christ our Saviour will not have spent its force in this world, but will continue to operate, and perchance to operate under more favourable conditions, in the world on which we enter when we pass through the gate and vestibule of death.  In short, the implication of these passages is, that all the familiar but august forces which are working together for the regeneration of the race here will continue to work hereafter, and surely to work with new power and happier effects in a world so much more advanced and spiritual than this.

On the other hand, these same Scriptures speak of an " æonial fire," an " æonial judgment," an " æonial punishment," an "æonial pruning;" and so convey the impression that in the ages to come there will be a revelation of the severity, as well as of the mercy, of God; a revelation of his burning wrath and indignation against all unrighteousness of men, as well as of his love and grace toward all that is righteous in them. But, if we would interpret these hints of terror aright, we must remember that, even here and now, God judgeth the righteous and God is angry with the wicked every day, yes, and angry with the righteous too.[1] Even here and now He is for ever judging us, if we do not judge ourselves, ever punishing, pruning, and chastising us for our good, and that we may bring forth more fruit. So that we must not hastily conclude that, in the ages to come, judgment and chastisement and punishment will change their very nature, and work to opposite effects. Analogy would rather suggest that then as now, there as here, God will still judge us in order that we may learn to judge ourselves, still chastise us for our good, still prune us that we may bring forth more fruit; and that the fire of his holy wrath against evil will burn up, or burn out, only that which has become evil in us, but liberate and enfranchise that which is good. And this suggestion is confirmed, as we shall see, by many direct teachings of Holy Writ.

[1] Psalm vii. 11, where "*with the wicked*" is, and is marked as, an interpolation.

What the Scriptures further teach concerning our conditions in the ages to come may perhaps be summed up under these three heads: (1) That as there are degrees of bliss in Paradise, so also there are degrees of punishment in Gehenna: (2) that as the reward of the righteous is at once retributive and perfecting, so the punishment of the unrighteous is at once retributive and remedial: and (3) that both to the righteous and to the unrighteous there will be vouchsafed a new and deeper revelation of the grace of God in Christ Jesus.

(1.) *There are degrees of bliss, or reward, in Paradise, and degrees of punishment in Gehenna.* We often speak of "fraternity and equality" as though the one were the complement or consequence of the other; whereas for anything like a true fraternity inequality is indispensable. "All men are brothers"? Yes; but let some be older and some younger, some more and some less experienced, some wiser and some less wise, some stronger and some less strong, some more and some less good; or what becomes of the variety and interest of human life? what becomes of its most tender and generous intercourses and ministrations? If every man were simply a repetition of every other, how sick we should soon grow of one another and of ourselves! how weary of looking at each other and seeing ourselves reflected from every face! If there were none to whom we could look up with reverence and admiration, and none to whom we could reach down a kind hand of help; if there were none to whom we could give and none from whom we could receive, nearly all that makes life vital to us and worth having would be gone. Yet how often have we conceived of the life to come as a dead level of guilt and pain, on the one hand, and, on the other, of goodness and bliss, with no inequalities in it, no variety, and, I had almost said, no interest.

Not thus, however, is the Paradise of God depicted in the Word; not thus, even the Gehenna of God. Our Lord Himself teaches us that they who have been faithful in a few things shall be made rulers over many things, while those who have been faithful in many shall receive the more.[1] And St Paul, in that strange weird passage[2] in which he tells the Corinthians how he was caught up into Paradise, affirms that he penetrated as far as to "the *third* heaven." But if there be a *third* heaven in Paradise, must there not also be a *second* and a *first*? May there not be, as the Jews held there were, *seven* heavens, each with its distinctive conditions and discipline and blessedness? May there not even be an infinite number of heavens, according to that promise of our

[1] St Luke xix. 12-26.    [2] 2 Corinthians xii. 2-4.

Lord,[1] in which He assures us that He has gone before us to prepare for each of us "his own place," *i.e.*, a place specially adapted to our personal bent and requirements?

In like manner, and with equal plainness, we are taught that Gehenna is as various as Paradise. Some that have done evil are to be beaten with few stripes, others with many stripes;[2] and, by the by, on the current doctrine of the future life, what is to be done with those who are to be beaten with few stripes *after they have received them*? And, again, our Lord[3] warned those who blindly followed the blind guidance of the Scribes that a heavy sentence would be passed upon them; but He threatened a still "severer sentence," a heavier judgment, on the Scribes themselves.

This variety of conditions in the future estate both of the righteous and of the unrighteous is, indeed, the simplest inference from that law of Retribution of which I have so often had to speak in these Lectures, and shall have to speak again immediately. For if every man is to receive the due reward of his deeds, and of *all* his deeds, "both good and bad," the life to come *must* be at least as various, as complex, as full of subtlely blended forces and interests as the life we now live in the flesh.

---

[1] St John xiv. 2.   [2] St Luke xii. 47, 48.   [3] St Mark xii. 40.

(2.) In the spiritual world *the reward of the righteous is at once retributive and perfecting, and the punishment of the unrighteous at once retributive and remedial.* On the former of these two points few words will suffice. For we all admit that the law of the future life which is most clearly revealed in Scripture is the law of Retribution; we all hope that by the discipline of that life, by its very blessedness, we may be more and more perfectly conformed to the image of Him that created us, until we are "satisfied with his likeness." And we can all see, I think, that if in that future life we *should* receive according to all our deeds, the very retribution that will come on us for our evil deeds, will be a most welcome discipline in holiness. In banishing all pain from the heavenly world, we too much forget how wholesome and blessed even pain may be, how it changes its very nature according as we view it and meet it. To be punished for a bad deed, to be compelled to reap what he has sown and to eat the fruit of his own doings, is terrible for a bad man, no doubt; but is it so terrible to a man who has repented his sin, who knows himself to be forgiven, and who longs to be delivered from the power of sin, to be quit of it at any cost? While we are on earth at all events, even when we know that our sin is forgiven and that God is making us pure, we are not let off from the painful consequences of our sins, and cannot be, since it is by enduring those consequences that we get the very discipline which detaches us from our sins and trains us in righteousness. And when, strengthened by a sense of the Divine love and forgiveness, we set ourselves to undo what we have done amiss, to arrest the evil forces we have set in motion, to replace them by good influences, we suffer much and long from shame, we are pierced with an infinite regret, as we discover how much harm we have done, and how much of it has gone beyond our reach so that we cannot arrest it. Even the risen Jesus bore in his side and hands and feet the stigmata, the marks of the wounds He had received in his conflict with sin: and, in like manner, even when we have renounced and in some measure subdued the lusts that war against the soul, we still bear about these "marks of the Lord Jesus," these traces, which often smart and throb painfully enough, of our former bondage to evil and of our present conflict with it. But if we take this discipline with a patient and hopeful heart, because we feel that God Himself is touched with a feeling of our infirmities and sorrows, because we feel that He is afflicted in our afflictions and is helping us to bear all we have to bear, and to do all we have to do, and is doing for us what we cannot do for ourselves, and loving and comforting us under all our pains and endeavours,—is our pain all pain ? do we not find in it a welcome discipline in holiness ? do we not even enter into a blessedness compared with which mere joys of sense are gross and poor ; do we not count *this* among our most precious spiritual experiences? And if it should prove that our future life is at once a continuation and a correction of our present life; if in the ages to come God should permit us to do rightly what we have here done wrongly; if He should permit us to undo the harm we have done, to do good to those to whom we had done evil, and to wipe out the very memory of our offences by a willing and cheerful obedience to the very laws we had broken: will not *that* be a delight to us, and an unspeakable solace, and a most exquisite blessedness? And suppose, also, we receive strength to be and do all that we desired to be and do here : to say the kind words we wished to say but could not find a tongue to utter, to shew the tender tremulous sympathies and affections we felt but were unable to express, to achieve the great things for God and man which we aspired but were unable to do, through some thwarting of nature or circumstance, some defect of character or will ;—will there not be in this a new and still vaster field of blessedness ?

And, again, how can we grow like God without entering into his eternal passion ? He is afflicted in all the afflictions of men, pained by all their sins, grieved in all their griefs. May we not hope, then, must we not hope, that hereafter this spirit of Divine Charity will more fully possess us, so that *we* shall be most truly afflicted by all that afflicts Him, and set ourselves to remedy all the wrongs over which He mourns, and to win back to righteousness those who, by their unrighteousness, grieve Him to the very heart? Is not this at least a nobler—yes, and even a happier—conception of the heavenly life than we have been wont to entertain? And may we not well believe that, when this muddy vesture of decay is stripped from our spirits, and we gain by that very loss new and enlarged powers of expression and action, we may be engaged in such blessed toils and honourable ministries as these?

On the other hand, we have clear reason for believing that the punishment of the unrighteous will be at once retributive and remedial. That they will suffer for their sins, and continue to suffer till they shake off their sins, follows both from the very nature of sin and of the human spirit, and from that great law of Retribution so plainly revealed both in human life and in the Inspired Word. God is merciful; but He never ceases to denounce tribulation, anguish, and woe on all that do evil. Nay, the Psalmist affirms that He is merciful *because* He renders unto every man according to his work:[1] though how that should be, unless retribution is designed to restore and save men, it is not easy to comprehend. We need not try to comprehend it. The Scriptures reveal in the simplest and most generous terms the true function and design of punishment. They say that, while the fathers of our flesh may chastise us after their pleasure,—without consideration, *i.e.*, or without due consideration, out of mere caprice or vindictiveness, not aiming at our welfare or from a mistaken conception of that wherein our welfare consists and the reasonable methods of securing it,—the Father of our Spirits chastises us only for our profit. And what profit? "That we may be partakers of his holiness."

Does any man say, "But that rule only holds in this world, not in the world to come?" We reply not only with an "Who art thou, O man, that thou shouldest limit the express words of Scripture and the boundless compassion of God?" but also by referring him to the very words of our Lord. *He* speaks even of the unrighteous who stand on his left hand, and whom He Himself has sentenced to "the æonial fire prepared for the devil and his angels," as leaving his bar to enter into an "æonial pruning," just as the righteous leave it to enter into æonial life; *He* declares that "*every one* shall be salted with fire;" and

[1] Psalm lxii. 12.

that surely can hardly mean less than that in every case the fire of the Divine wrath is to have a preservative, a sanitary and sanctifying, effect. Nay, more, we ask such an one to go down with us into Gehenna, and to mark the effect of its torment on one poor soul long since adjudged to it. The rich man of our Lord's parable—Dives, as we call him, though Tradition speaks of him as Nimeusis—had thought mainly of himself and the pampering of his senses while he was on earth; and nevertheless had comfortably assumed that he was all the while a true and faithful child of Abraham, and would lie "in Abraham's bosom" when he had to doff his purple and fine linen and could no longer enjoy his sumptuous fare. But mark the change that has passed on him ere he has been more than a little while in Hades. No sooner does he lift up his eyes on the new scene into which he has passed than he awakes to a sense of his real position, and discovers that, instead of being in Abraham's bosom, he is in torment; that, instead of being near and dear to Abraham and to Abraham's God, he is far off from them, alienated from their life through sin that is in him. He is taught to correct the false estimate of good and evil things which he had framed and on which he had acted, by the discovery that what he had held to be "good things" had landed him in Gehenna, while what he had held to be "evil things" had carried Lazarus into Abraham's bosom. He is taught to replace superstition by religion; to look for spiritual instruction and impression not to apparitions, not to the reappearance of one risen from the dead, but to the divine law written on the heart and interpreted by Moses and the prophets. And the moral effect of these lessons and discoveries is that, instead of thinking only or mainly of himself, he begins to think of others, of his five brethren; and that instead of longing that they may receive what he had been wont to think the good things of life, such as sumptuous raiment and sumptuous fare, he craves that they may be spared that torment of a wasted life of which he has become conscious, and be saved unto life eternal. Now if we are to take this parable as an illustration of the future lot of the wicked, we see here what the discipline of Gehenna is to be, and what its fruits. And who that has an eye to see the lessons which this rich man had been taught by the very torment of Gehenna, and a heart to appreciate the happy moral change it had wrought upon him, burning out his selfishness and worldliness, and quickening at least the germs of charity and spirituality within him,—who can doubt that that discipline is designed for "the correction and bettering of the offender," that the very torments of the wicked are designed to redeem and restore them?

And, in part at least, we can see *how* it should be so, how the change from this world to the next should involve the keenest torment to the unrighteous and yet the most effectual discipline. Think for a moment what the punishment, and what the revelation, of merely having his body stripped off him must be to a man who has walked after the flesh, and not after the spirit. He has lived mainly to pamper the senses, or to gratify the passions and cravings which hold by sense, or to secure the means for gratifying them. In his pursuit and enjoyment of the things which are seen and temporal, he has neglected, he has become insensible to the things which are unseen and eternal. But when he himself becomes an unclothed spirit, he can be unconscious of them and indifferent to them no longer. They press in upon him from every side. The veil of sense and sensuous pursuits has fallen from his eyes; he is in the real world now, not the phenomenal, and he can no longer look out upon it through eyes of flesh. And, moreover, he has lost all that he most loved and with which he was most familiar, all that he deemed to be his "good things." He who counted for so much in this world counts for nothing in that. All his pleasures are gone, all his gains, all his pursuits. He is torn by appetites and cravings which can no longer be indulged. All the conditions of his life are strange, unwelcome, repugnant to him; there has been little in the past to prepare him for them, much to unfit him for them. Can he fail to be devoured by a sense of loss and misery, by shame for the past, by dread of what is to come, by a horrible sense of discord between himself and all that is good and fair and enduring? Can he fail to feel that he is far off from the God from whom he has long alienated himself, and feel it so keenly as to make any place a place of torment to him? And yet who does not see that in the very shame and misery produced by a revelation of that which is spiritual, and of his alienation from it, and of his guilt in neglecting it, lies his one chance of redemption? All that was familiar to him is seen in a new light, and a light which compels him to reverse his former estimates of good and evil. All that was invisible and distant here becomes near and visible there; and the man, since he can no longer hide himself from spiritual realities, but is compelled to dwell among them and to brood over them, may find in his very punishment the means of spiritual life. He may begin to study what is highest in himself and best, in place of that which is lowest and worst; he may begin to think of others instead of himself and to study how they may be kept from a torment like his own. And who will venture to say that God will destroy a spirit in whom these germs of the Divine Life have been liberated and developed?

(3). In the age or ages to come *there will be accorded a new and deeper revelation of the grace of God in Christ Jesus, a new and more penetrating proclamation of the Gospel.* In its essence, the Gospel is a manifestation of the loving and redeeming will of God. It culminates in the gift and sacrifice of his Son; for here we see most clearly how far He will go and how much He will do to save men from their sins. But when we considered the doctrine of Redemption, we agreed that even the sacrifice of Christ was but a manifestation within the bounds of time and space of the eternal passion of the Father; that, because God is unchangeable, He must always be what we see Him to be at any moment; and that, therefore, the love He manifested for sinful men in the sacrifice of Christ must always be in his nature, and must continue to manifest itself, in appropriate forms, through all the ages and changes of time. To doubt that, is to doubt that God is the same yesterday, to-day, and for ever. In what forms He will manifest his redeeming love for men in the ages to come, we may not be able to conceive. We could not have conceived beforehand how He would manifest it to the ancient world, in the age that is past,—that, before Christ came, He would have foreshadowed it by that strange system of sacrifices by which He enabled Abraham and the faithful of his seed to see the day and the work of Christ afar off. We need not wonder, therefore, if we fail to imagine how, in what forms of light and grace, He will reveal that redeeming Love in the ages to be. But we must not, and cannot, doubt that, in some form, He will reveal it. Indeed we have in Scripture itself proofs as well as hints that He will reveal it both to the righteous and to the unrighteous, and even one very broad hint as to how He will reveal it.

That a new and deeper revelation of the loving and redeeming will of God will be vouchsafed to the righteous, you are doubtless prepared to admit. Nevertheless, glance at two passages[1] which, when combined, may define and confirm your hope. In writing to the Colossians, St Paul, speaking of the risen and glorified Christ, affirms that "in Him all the fulness of the Godhead has its fixed abode *bodily*," or, rather, "*bodily-wise*;" that is to say, the Apostle affirms that in some mysterious way Christ has carried our entire human nature, body as well as soul, into the heavenly places; that He still retains that power of physical manifestation which He used more than once after He had risen from the dead, and even after He had gone up into heaven—as St Stephen and St Paul and St John all attest: in short, that He still wears, or can still assume, the spiritual but human

---

[1] Colossians ii. 9; and St John xvii. 24.

body of his resurrection. And our Lord Himself, when praying to his Father for his disciples says: "Father, I will that they also whom Thou hast given me be with me where I am, *that they may behold my glory.*" Christ, then, retains the power of revealing Himself "bodily-wise" to men, and asks that his disciples may join Him in the world to come in order that they may "see his glory." Did you ever consider what it may be to behold Christ in his glory? If you have, you surely were not so childish as to suppose that you were to see Him standing as in the centre of the sun, irradiated by and emitting intolerable rays of splendour! The glory of Christ is a spiritual glory, the glory of a perfect wisdom and a perfect love, wisdom and love in active exercise, revealing themselves with a divine energy and power. We see Him manifesting forth his glory as we read the Gospels, and would give much no doubt to look for a moment on his very face, to see one of his mighty works, to listen to one of his gracious words. But why should we frame so poor a wish as that when, in the ages to come, we are to see a whole new Gospel enacted before our eyes,—to see Him "bodily-wise" yet in his glory; not dumb and inert, but speaking words that will quicken life and clothing Himself in the loveliness of perfect deeds?

This new and more glorious Incarnation, this new

and more glorious Revelation, may be denied to the unrighteous who are receiving the due reward of their sinful deeds; for of them it is written that, at least for a time, they shall be "destroyed from the presence of Christ and the glory of his power:" and that *may* mean that the glorious revelation vouchsafed to the redeemed will be denied to them, and denied simply because as yet they are unable to receive it. But it does not follow that all manifestations of the redeeming mercy of God will be refused them. Christ in the severity of his anger against sin, Christ in the tenderness of his grace to sinners, may be visible to those who would only be dazzled and blinded by Christ in the full glory of his power. And if God has once shewn that He will make any sacrifice for the salvation of the guilty, must not that be always true of Him? must He not continue to manifest his blended severity and mercy in the ages to come? Has He not, in that long and splendid catena of passages which I recited to you in my last Lecture, declared it to be his intention to recover the whole human race to righteousness and peace, to prove Himself "the Saviour of all men?" If He is to be the Saviour of *all* men, must He not redeem even most of the men who have passed across the face of the earth *after* they have left the earth? And have we not at least one instance recorded in which Christ entered into the vast Hadean kingdom and preached his Gospel to them that were lost? Did He not, when "He descended into Hades," preach it with such power that even the vilest sinners of the ancient world, every imagination of whose hearts had been only evil continually, were constrained to listen and respond, to rise and follow Him over the "great gulf," on the bridge of his cross, into the fair gardens and spacious halls of Paradise? Does not the Apostle Peter expressly affirm, "for *this* cause was the gospel preached also to them that were dead . . . that they might live according to God in the spirit," even while their fellows on earth still accounted them to be dead in trespasses and sins? And if the Gospel has been preached in Hades once, and so preached as that the worst of men were saved by it, why may it not be preached there again and again, and preached with results still larger and happier?

When it is preached again, it may be that Christ will not be the preacher, or not the only preacher. For when we considered the true doctrine of Election we concluded that as one man had always been chosen for the good of other men, one family for the good of all families, one nation for the good of all nations, so also it might be—nay, must be—in the ages to come. If, then, we are of those who have been chosen and redeemed, it may be that *we* shall be the happy messengers of God's love and mercy to those who are still being purged from their sins,—thus entering at once into the eternal passion of God and into the redeeming work of Christ; being afflicted, like the Father, in all the sins and afflictions of the unrighteous, and, like Christ, descending into the very Pit if by any means we may save some. It may be through *our* ministry that the purpose of God will be accomplished, that all Israel will be saved and the fulness of the Gentiles brought in. God grant that it may be so! for that surely would be an infinitely diviner service and reward than to sit, clothed in white raiment, striking harps of gold.

The Scriptures, then, have much to teach us of the *future*, though not much of the *final*, estate of men. And what they teach, in so far at least as we have been able to gather it up, comes to this. No man is wholly good, no man wholly bad. Still some men may fairly be called good on the whole, although much sin and imperfection still cleaves to them; and others may fairly be called bad on the whole, although there is still much in them that is good, and still more which is capable of becoming good. When we die, we shall all receive the due recompense of our deeds, of all our deeds, whether they have been good or whether they have been bad. If, by the grace of God, we have been good on the whole, we may hope to rise into a large and happy spiritual kingdom in which all that is pure and noble and kind in us will develop into new vigour and clothe itself with new beauty; in which also we shall find the very discipline we need in order that we may be wholly purged from sin and imperfection; in which we may undo much that we have done wrongly, do again and with perfect grace that which we have done imperfectly, become what we have wished and aimed to be, achieve what we have longed to achieve, attain the wisdom, the gifts and powers and graces to which we have aspired: in which, above all, we may be engaged in errands of usefulness and compassion by which the purpose of the Divine love and grace will be fully accomplished. If we have been bad on the whole, we may hope—and we ought to *hope* for it—to pass into a painful discipline so keen and searching that we shall become conscious of our sins and feel that we are only receiving the due reward of them; but, since there has been some good in us, and this good is capable of being drawn out and disentangled from the evil which clouded and marred it, we may also hope, by the very discipline and torment of our spirits, to be led to repentance, and, through repentance, unto life: we may hope that the disclosures of the spiritual world will take a spiritual effect upon us, gradually raising and renewing us till we too are prepared to enter the Paradise of God and behold the presence of the Lord and the glory of his power: we may hope that our friends who have already been redeemed will pity us and minister to us, bringing us not simply a cup of cold water to cool our tongue, but words of instruction and life. And as for the great mass of our fellowmen, we may hope and believe that those who have had no chance of salvation here will have one there; that those who have had a poor chance will get a better one: that those who have had a good chance and lost it will get a new but a severer chance, and even as they suffer the inevitable results of their folly and sin will feel

> the hands
> That reach through darkness, moulding men.

This, on the whole, I take to be the teaching of Scripture concerning the lot of men in the age to come,—a teaching which enables us to see "beneath the abyss of hell a bottomless abyss of love." And if it clash with some dogmas that we have held and some interpretations which are familiar to us, it nevertheless accords, not with "the mind of Christ" only, but also with the dictates of Reason and Conscience, the voices of God within the soul. It presents no such sudden break in our life as, in the teeth of all probability, we have been wont to conceive ; no heaven for which we feel that even the best of us must be unfit, no hell which is a monstrous offence to our sense of justice. It promises to every man the mercy of justice, of a due reward for all he has been and done ; and, while it impresses on us the utter hatefulness and misery of sin, it holds out to every one of us the prospect of being redeemed from all sin and uncleanness by that just God who is also a Saviour. Nor does it less accord with the demands of Science than with the dictates of Reason and the Moral Sense ; for it carries on the evolution of the human race through all the ages to come. And, therefore, let others think as they will, and cherish what trust they will: " *but* " as for us, with the Apostle of the Gentiles, our own Apostle, "*we trust in the living God who is the Saviour of all men.*"

www.ingramcontent.com/pod-product-compliance
Lightning Source LLC
Chambersburg PA
CBHW021808230426
43669CB00008B/677